THE UNOFFICIAL GUIDE TO LIFE AFTER HIGH SCHOOL

Len Woods

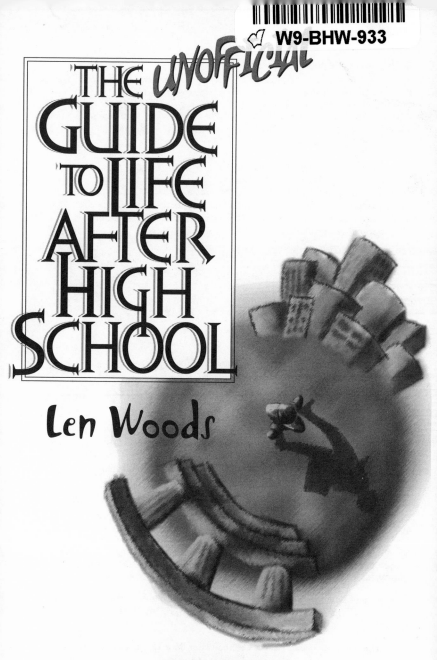

Baker Books

A Division of Baker Book House Co
Grand Rapids, Michigan 49516

© 1998 by Len Woods

Published by Baker Books
a division of Baker Book House Company
P.O. Box 6287, Grand Rapids, MI 49516-6287

Paperback edition published 2000

Printed in the United States of America

Library of Congress Cataloging-in-Publication Data

Woods, Len.
    The unofficial guide to life after high school / Len Woods.
        p.   cm.
    ISBN 0-8010-1158-2 (cloth)
    ISBN 0-8010-6208-X (paper)
    1. High school graduates—Conduct of life. 2. Young adults—
Conduct of life. I. Title.
BJ1661.W64   1998
170'.44—dc21   97-18260

For current information about all releases from Baker Book House, visit our web
site:
                    http://www.bakerbooks.com

To

the students

of The Fellowship

at Louisiana Tech—

I'm so glad God

brought me to you

and you to me.

Thank you for a wonderful

seven years.

CONTENTS

ACKNOWLEDGMENTS 6

INTRODUCTION 7

Truths about Life

1   LIFE IS HARD 12

2   LIFE ISN'T FAIR 15

3   WHEN TRUTH IS REJECTED,
     LIFE BECOMES UNLIVABLE 18

4   LIFE REQUIRES A CERTAIN
     AMOUNT OF INTOLERANCE 22

5   LIFE IS SHORTER THAN YOU THINK 25

Truths about People

6   PEOPLE HAVE INFINITE WORTH 30

7   PEOPLE ARE NOT BASICALLY GOOD 33

8   NOBODY HAS IT TOGETHER 36

9   NOBODY GETS AWAY WITH ANYTHING 39

10   PEOPLE WERE CREATED
     FOR RELATIONSHIPS 41

Truths about You

11   YOU DON'T KNOW EVERYTHING 46

12   YOU CAN MEASURE YOUR SPIRITUAL
MATURITY BY HOW WELL YOU LOVE 49

13   YOU NEED THE CHURCH ALMOST AS MUCH
AS THE CHURCH NEEDS YOU 52

14   YOU WILL BE EITHER A CHRISTIAN WHO
CONSUMES OR A CHRISTIAN WHO COMMITS 56

15   YOU DON'T *HAVE* TO SIN 59

Truths about God

16   GOD IS GOOD 64

17   GOD REQUIRES YOU TO "OWN" YOUR OWN
FAITH 67

18   LOVING GOD IS *THE* GREAT PRIORITY OF LIFE 70

19   ONLY GOD CAN FILL THE HOLE IN YOUR SOUL 73

20   GOD HAS DEFEATED OUR GREAT ENEMY 76

Truths about the Rest of Your Life

21   GOOD THINGS COME TO THOSE WHO WAIT 82

22   GOOD THINGS COME TO THOSE WHO WORK 85

23   TODAY WILL HAPPEN ONLY ONCE 88

24   CONFLICTS DON'T MAGICALLY GO AWAY 90

25   IT'S NEVER TOO LATE TO TURN AROUND 94

ACKNOWLEDGMENTS

I WISH TO THANK:

- *Ray "Raybert" McKinney and Jeannie Gunter—the two greatest interns in the history of the human race.*

- *Brian "B. Dubbs" Wells—"The game ends too soon, you know?"*

- *Carrie Love—I'm proud of you!*

- *Peter Wallace—my dear friend who lives much too far away.*

- *Jan and Steve—for being there for me during all my college years!*

- *Ronnie, Candy, Brent, and Lance—for loving and believing in me.*

- *Dan Van't Kerkhoff, Melinda Van Engen, and the troops at Baker—for giving me the chance to put into words the deepest convictions of my heart.*

- *Dr. Larry Crabb—a man I know only through his writings but who has marked my life in profound ways.*

- *And most of all, Cindi, my (sweet and gorgeous) bride, and Walter and Jack, my (fun and funny) sons.*

INTRODUCTION

The details vary, but the basic ceremony is always the same.

Dangling tassels. Congratulatory speeches by people with names like "The Honorable Mortimer Hollingsworth." Valedictory addresses filled with metaphors about "soaring like eagles on the winds of possibility." The fear of tripping in front of a giant audience. A short walk, often up a flight of steep steps. A handshake or two. More video cameras rolling than during a papal visit. Your *full* name announced over the PA system. The embarrassing yells of a loudmouthed relative. Then the prize . . . a robed arm extends to you a hard-earned diploma. Flashbulbs. A few final remarks by Principal Smeltzer. The grand recessional. Lots of tears and hugs.

What does it all mean?

For one thing, graduation means you finally get to take off that sweaty polyester gown. It also means raking in some great gifts (by one friend's calculations, .4 presents for every announcement sent out). Actually, despite all the hoopla, graduation means you've mastered (maybe *survived* is a better word) a certain number of required high school courses. It means you have been given (at least theoretically) the basic educational skills our society says you need to possess. For example:

- *You now know that the only person in the world who actually understands the so-called "literary classics" is some guy named Cliff.*

- *You have grasped the intricacies and applications of the Pythagorean theorem (that earlier code of laws voted down when Congress approved the Magna Carta in 1911).*

- *You are the author of a smokin' research paper on Boyle's law. (Remember Boyle? The scientist who accidentally discovered boiling water and then invented hot pads?)*

I won't kid you—it's not going to be easy to learn lessons more useful than *those!* But you will. Because now comes the fun part. At long last you get to leave behind high school academia. Whether you get a job, go to college, or join the armed services, you finally get to launch out into the classroom of real life.

"The classroom of real life? You mean I have to keep learning?!"

You betcha! The notion that your education is over when you graduate is a widespread myth. In truth, the really good stuff is just ahead—all those mysterious realities they never taught you in high school. So even if you're finished with your *formal* training, you still have to go to school—the school of real life.

This brings to mind a second myth common among high school grads: The important realities of life can come to us only through negative personal experiences. Perhaps you've heard friends say, "I can't follow your advice. I need to learn my own lessons, in my own way." (Maybe you've even said this yourself!) No offense, but let me just say, "This is not the smartest way to live."

I have a friend who frequently says to me, "I'm going to school off you." What he means is he's watching me, trying to learn from both my successes and failures. When I do something foolish and reap the consequences, he makes a mental note: "I'm sure not going to make *that* mistake!" When I do something right and experience blessing, he files that away too. He's being wise. He's trying to avoid unnecessary heartache.

That is why, I guess, I wrote this book. I don't want you to suffer avoidable pain in the infamous "school of hard knocks." I'd much rather you go to school off me and the handful of students I have described in these pages.

THE **UNOFFICIAL**

Look at this book as a kind of basic preparatory manual for the rest of your life—exactly like those delightful manuals designed to get you ready for big exams such as the SAT or ACT, only with these minor differences:

COLLEGE PREP MANUAL	THE Unofficial GUIDE TO LIFE AFTER HIGH SCHOOL
• As thick as a big city phone book	> A slim 96 pages
• Requires a calculator and #2 pencil	> Nothing else required
• Assumes you know algebra	> Assumes you can count to twenty-five
• Brain draining	> Soul stirring
• Discouraging	> Encouraging
• Can help you get into college	> Can help you *stay* in college (and enjoy it!)
• Has nothing to do with real life	> All about real life
• Hypothetical word problems	> True stories
• Makes a terrible graduation gift	> Makes a great graduation gift
• Information becomes dated quickly	> Timeless wisdom from God's Word
• Positively will *not* make you smile	> Might make you laugh

I hope something in these pages will prove helpful to you. Congratulations on all you've accomplished in high school and best wishes for all that lies ahead in the school of real life.

I

LIFE IS HARD

*Yet man is born to trouble as surely
as sparks fly upward.*

JOB 5:7

Ron went to bed last night in a great mood. Twenty-four hours later he could not be in a worse mood. When asked to put words to his feelings, he replied: "Angry, cheated . . ." (plus a few other choice remarks we can't print here!).

What happened to prompt such a mood swing?

Nothing of a life-and-death nature, just a whole series of frustrating yet fairly common events. His roommate let him oversleep and he missed an eight o'clock class (featuring a quiz he won't be able to make up). At lunch, he discovered a fifteen-dollar parking ticket on his car, courtesy of the campus police. A book supposedly on reserve in the library was missing, meaning he couldn't complete an important assignment. A notice from the bank arrived in the mail: He had recently bounced two checks! Now, just past midnight, Ron realizes he's facing at least two hours' worth of accounting home-work. And all he wants to do is go to bed.

Ah, college life! Ah, life, *period*.

What do we do when we have days like Ron's? Obviously, we can't control our circumstances, but isn't there *something* we can do to minimize our mood swings?

Yes. One thing—perhaps the best thing—we can do is remember one simple truth: Life is hard. It's been this way ever since our forefathers Adam and Eve turned their backs on God (Genesis 3). Foolishly they thought they could improve on paradise. Consequently, they plunged themselves and the entire human race into sin and misery. Eden was lost. The result is that we now live in what theologians call a "fallen" world, a place where circumstances go wrong far more often than they go right. From potholes to earthquakes, from dieting to death, we are reminded daily—if we're at all perceptive—of just how flawed things really are. As author and psychologist Larry Crabb has said, "In a fallen world, there is something wrong with everything."

Life is hard. In our saner moments we recognize that reality. The problem comes during our "insane" moments when we forget it.

If you wake up expecting to have a trouble-free day, you are setting yourself up for major disappointment. *Nobody* hits every green light, encounters only nice people, or gets only the easiest and most fascinating professors. On the contrary, in a fallen world, cafeteria trays occasionally slip from your grasp, knee cartilage tears, and dorm neighbors play loud music just when you really need to sleep.

I am not encouraging you to become a pessimist or to adopt a doom-and-gloom philosophy that says life is terrible. It is *not* terrible. Our daily experience still contains wonderful moments of sheer joy (see chap. 23). Our gracious God regularly fills our lives with good gifts (James 1:17). We can and should enjoy these blessings.

But we also need to be realists. We do not live in Eden. We live in a world marred by the terrible effects of the fall. We must shed the illusion that life *now* is supposed to be easy and carefree. We must get rid of the unrealistic expectation that we will somehow be able to cruise through life untouched by pain or difficulty.

Once we come to terms with this truth, we are better able to endure the trials and problems we face. Knowing that life is hard doesn't make bad times fun, just less devastating. A relational breakup still hurts like crazy, a bout with mono is still a drag. But these kinds of setbacks don't shock us. We recognize that for the time being, we have no choice but to take the bad with the good.

And so that we don't lose hope, we keep in mind another truth: God is in the process of redeeming and restoring all of his creation. Revelation speaks of "new heavens and a new earth," an environment free from pain and suffering and tears and death. That's where those who know Christ are headed—back to paradise.

THE **UNOFFICIAL**

2

LIFE ISN'T FAIR

*I have observed something else in
this world of ours. The fastest runner
doesn't always win the race, and the
strongest warrior doesn't always win
the battle. The wise are often poor, and the
skillful are not necessarily wealthy. . . .
It is all decided by chance.*

ECCLESIASTES 9:11 NLT

During my senior year at Louisiana State University, I took a class in journalism law. It was one of the tougher courses in my curriculum, covering hundreds of court cases involving first amendment rights and the press.

The night before our first big exam (one of only two that semester), my girlfriend and I had a major misunderstanding. I don't remember exactly what our disagreement was about, but I do recall that I was too upset to study.

So tossing aside my lecture notes, I headed back over to my girlfriend's dorm. We ended up talking until four in the morning! Afterwards I felt better about us, but I also felt physically exhausted and emotionally spent.

Driving home, I remembered my exam—less than

four hours away. I wasn't even close to being ready, and I knew I couldn't possibly get ready. So I hastily concocted what I thought was a perfect plan: My professor had office hours before our 8:00 A.M. class. I would go to the journalism building at 7:30 and tell him the truth about my late night lovers' quarrel. Surely, as a married man, he would understand. (He would probably even admire my strong commitment to immediate conflict resolution.) I would tell him of my fervent desire not only to understand the intricacies of journalism law but also to do well in his class. Then I would look him in the eye and humbly ask for a makeup exam later in the week when I was rested and ready.

Confident I had a reasonable case to make, I marched into his office three hours later. As I began my well-rehearsed speech, I sensed he was unimpressed. When I got to the part about a makeup exam, he cut me off.

"Look, I'm sorry about your personal problems, but I can't give you a makeup exam for that." Then, glancing at his watch, he added curtly, "The test isn't for another twenty minutes. I suggest you use that time to go someplace and study."

Staggering out into the hall, I remember thinking about all the people I knew at LSU who had seriously unhealthy dating relationships and never made even the slightest effort to improve them! I thought about all the students I knew who routinely goofed off and then cheated on exams! What about the ones who told outrageous lies to their instructors in order to get makeup tests?! One phrase kept ringing in my mind: Life isn't fair!

Guess what? In that sleep-deprived moment, I was in touch with a profound truth. Life is *not* fair. Because we live in a fallen world (remember chap. 1?), things are often extremely unjust.

A hard-working teacher struggles ten to twelve hours a day to make a difference at an inner-city high school and gets paid a paltry twenty-five thousand dollars a year. A mediocre jock with an attitude makes that much (or more) for playing a few minutes in one game! The beautiful airhead has guys lining up to take her out. The God-loving girl with normal looks sits home. Powerful people play favorites. People with connections pull strings.

Isn't that the way of the world? Bad people often get ahead. Good people often suffer. Chances are you've experienced this hard truth already. Without question, you'll bump up against it again and again in the days to come.

So the question becomes: What do you do when you're staring an "unfair" situation in the face? How do you respond when someone less qualified gets the scholarship you deserve? Or when you get laid off from a job when you had been working your tail off?

First, it's important to remember that though life may be unfair, God never is. His nature is just (Deut. 32:4). The Lord can never be the source of unfairness in your life. Think about it: How could a just God cause injustice? Sometimes we assess situations prematurely, before they have completely unfolded. Like the time in college when my application to be part of a missionary team was turned down with no explanation. Was God being unfair? It seemed like it . . . until God used that rejection to open the door to a summer youth internship where I had the time of my life!

Second, remember that within his sovereign plan, God uses "unfair" situations to build character in us. Many people—perhaps most—in the face of injustice reveal their true colors. They whine and complain. They become bitter. They look for ethical and moral shortcuts. The reasoning? "If no one else is going to play by the rules, then I'm not going to either!"

Contrast this common reaction with the uncommon response of the biblical character Joseph (Genesis 37, 39–45). Sold into slavery by his own brothers, falsely accused of attempted rape, forgotten in a foreign prison, Joseph never once moaned about life's unfairness. He just kept doing the right thing. He clung to the belief that God is ultimately in control of all things and the related hope that one day some measure of justice would prevail in his life (Ps. 98:9; Luke 18:1–8). It did. It always does.

In retrospect, I look back on the incident of my journalism law exam and question whether *I* was being fair to my professor. Was it right for me to put him on the spot like that? Probably not.

At any rate, I crammed like crazy for fifteen minutes and somehow made an eighty on the test! Can you believe it? I was thrilled. For the second exam, I studied days in advance, for hours on end. I made an eighty-one. A measly one point improvement. Who ever said life is fair?

3

WHEN TRUTH IS REJECTED, LIFE BECOMES UNLIVABLE

In those days Israel had no king,
so the people did whatever seemed right
in their own eyes.

JUDGES 21:25 NLT

One day in a lecture on different cultures, my sociology professor casually made the statement, "And, of course, we all know that there are no absolutes—everything is relative."

I was startled. I glanced around for some kind of reaction. But there was none. No one protested or even raised an eyebrow. Most of my classmates just continued scribbling notes. I sat there for an eternal moment wondering what to do. *Should I say something? Do I let him get away with that statement?*

Reluctantly, I raised my hand. My heart was pounding. My mouth was dry.

"You have a question?"

"Well, with all due respect, sir, I have to take issue

with your statement about everything being relative and there being no absolutes."

"Oh, really?" My professor seemed to swell with energy, like a big cat preparing to pounce on a poor, dumb mouse. "Okay, why don't *you* give us an absolute?"

"Well," I gulped. "I happen to believe that the Bible is absolutely true."

Nodding with disdain, he smiled and snorted contemptuously. As if on cue, the class began to snicker.

I felt the sweat dripping from my armpits, but I pressed on. "I just know there *have* to be some absolutes. Because if everything is relative, then anything goes. If there is no ultimate standard of right and wrong, then why would it be bad for me—if I had a gun—to shoot you right now?" The class got strangely quiet, and I realized immediately that it probably wasn't a good idea to talk, even in abstract terms, about shooting your sociology professor! So I quickly changed analogies.

"What I mean is, if you take what you just said to its logical conclusion, then on what basis can we condemn Hitler for what he did? He was only doing what he felt was right. His culture went along with him. If everything is relative, how can you, or anyone else, judge what he did as 'wrong'? It's just your opinion against his."

What happened next is all a blur. I seem to recall that he made a couple of cracks designed to make me look like an idiot, the class laughed, and then he changed the subject. But the fact is he never really answered my questions. I don't think he *had* any answers.

We live in a generation that has embraced the belief system of my college sociology professor. The vast majority of young adults do not believe in the concept of absolute truth, that is, truth with a capital "T," truth that transcends time and cultures and applies to all people everywhere.

The result is a chaotic, confusing culture where relativism rules. And when truth is reduced to nothing more than individual preference, people are forced to rely on inadequate measuring sticks. Consider . . .

Some decide right and wrong by *personal opinion*. But what happens when my opinion collides with someone else's?

Others determine right and wrong by strong *feelings*. But feelings can be deceptive, even destructive. After all, the rapist *feels* like raping and the killer *feels* like killing.

What about *cultural norms*? Are they reliable? Not really. We've already
mentioned what happened in Hitler's Germany. A majority simply
means most of the people agree. But it's possible they are agreeing
about the wrong thing.

Is *law* a good indicator of right and wrong? Not necessarily. Consider the
laws in this country that used to permit slavery and prohibit women
from voting.

What about *science*? It's not always reliable either. Facts can be misinter-
preted. (Remember how you and your high school chemistry lab part-
ner reached totally different conclusions than everyone else in the
class?) Or they can be manipulated. Remember Piltdown Man? For
almost fifty years, paleontologists were certain a jawbone and skull
fragment found in England in 1912 were five-hundred-thousand-year-
old "proof" of our "ape-like" ancestors. In 1950, further testing
proved Piltdown Man to be a hoax. Someone had doctored a modern
ape's jaw and a human skull so as to produce the "evidence" they
were hoping to find to bolster their theories!

Expert opinion is inadequate as a guide for what is true, because the so-
called "experts" often disagree—violently.

The bottom line? As a philosophy, relativism is self-defeating. It can't sup-
port itself. If there are no absolutes, then not even that statement can be
regarded as absolutely true!

So what is our alternative? I propose absolutism—an ultimate, universal
standard of right and wrong. And how do we come up with that standard? We don't "come up with it." It "comes down to us." It
comes to us via revelation. God makes it known.

God has given us the historical Jesus, who said, "I
am . . . the truth" (John 14:6). He has also given
us the holy Scriptures about which Jesus
said, "Your word is truth" (John
17:17). In short, we have a living
Word and a written Word to carefully consider. Two radical Truth
claims. And if they are true, everything changes. If they are true,
they are true regardless of what
anyone feels or thinks. If they are

THE **UNOFFICIAL**

true in an absolute sense, then it must follow that much of what our culture says is false.

In our minds we know that two plus two cannot equal both four and seven. In our hearts we have an inherent idea of right and wrong. What else can explain the universal outrage for the sadistic serial killer who preys on helpless children? To paraphrase C. S. Lewis, we have an intrinsic sense that some moralities are better than others. Deep down we *do* believe in some sort of ultimate standard. Otherwise, we would never be able to make claims such as "That's not fair!" or "That's wrong!"

How do *you* determine what's true? Do your standards provide a coherent framework for life? If you reject the concept of absolute Truth, where do you intend to find ultimate meaning? No questions are more important than these.

4

LIFE REQUIRES A CERTAIN AMOUNT OF INTOLERANCE

People with open minds must be careful these days. There are a lot of others around who are intent on throwing rubbish into them.

SOURCE UNKNOWN

As you get ready to plunk down tens of thousands of dollars in tuition money over the next four years (five to ten years for some of you luckier readers), let me share with you a happy thought: Very little of the wisdom you will gain during your college experience will come from the lips of a lecturing professor.

This is an undeniable fact. Ask any graduate. I learned far more about human nature living in the dorm and watching reruns of *The Andy Griffith Show* than I ever did sitting through Psychology 101.

If you go to college, you *will* get an education, but it will come to you in unexpected ways. Consider three unrelated incidents that combined to teach me a crucial truth: Life requires a certain amount of intolerance.

- *Our intramural basketball team named The Magic Gerbils (honestly!) was playing a big game. Retrieving a loose ball near the edge of the court, I turned to dribble toward our basket. Suddenly the ref blew his whistle. He claimed I had stepped on the sideline. As if a couple of inches mattered! Like it hurt anybody!*
- *In a geology class, I got back an exam covered in red ink. A number of my multiple-choice answers had been marked wrong by some grad-school grader with rocks in his head. Why?! Those answers seemed perfectly logical and sensible to me.*
- *Late one night, my stomach began growling fiercely. I had no money and no car. What I did have was a bag of leftover fried chicken in my dorm refrigerator. This particular poultry had been in my refrigerator for a week—or maybe two, I wasn't sure. I only knew I was starving, and the chicken did not appear to have any visible growths on it. So I consumed it . . . quickly. A couple hours later my body rejected it . . . even more quickly.*

The truth I slowly grasped from these separate incidents is that we live in an intolerant world. But I also began to see that a certain amount of intolerance is a *necessary* thing—even a *good* thing.

Imagine basketball (or any sport) with no boundaries and no rules. Players dribbling into the bleachers to avoid a defender! Coaches claiming a player should be awarded points for hitting the rim because, after all, how much closer can you get?!

Imagine a math professor telling her engineering students before an exam: "Relax. Nobody's going to flunk. As long as you make a sincere effort to do your best, any and every answer is acceptable. Who am *I* to label someone's hard work as 'wrong'?"

Aren't you glad police don't allow motorists to drive the wrong way down a one-way street? I'm relieved to know that we have some very "narrow-minded" airline inspectors who are quick to ground any jet considered unsafe. And if I'm about to undergo surgery, I want my doctor to be extremely intolerant of germs, wouldn't you?

As the concept of absolute Truth has been abandoned by this generation (see chap. 3), it has become fashionable to accept all beliefs and behaviors as valid. And, in fact, anyone who suggests that certain ideas or actions are wrong is labeled narrow-minded, or worse.

But consider how absurd this "Religion of Tolerance" is . . . how impossible it is to live out in a consistent fashion:

STUDENT A: "I believe in tolerance, that we should accept *every* lifestyle and belief!"

STUDENT B: "So then, you would be willing to also accept Christianity, which speaks of absolute Truth, and which says some beliefs and behaviors are just simply wrong?"

STUDENT A: "No, I don't accept that."

STUDENT B: "But I thought you said you are tolerant of *all* beliefs, and that *all* are valid."

STUDENT A: "Um . . . not that one."

STUDENT B: "Aren't you contradicting yourself?"

STUDENT A: "Er, I, uh, I have to go to class."

Do you see the irony and inconsistency? Despite the steady drumbeat for "tolerance," our society is extremely intolerant. We all recognize that without certain agreed-upon standards, life quickly becomes chaotic. And without adherence to those standards, life can even be dangerous.

This is true not just in math class, on the football field, in the science lab, or in the E.R., but in all of life. In the same way that not just any food is acceptable for consumption, not all philosophies of life are healthy. Ideas have consequences. They lead to action. And bad beliefs have awful consequences because they lead to unhealthy behavior.

What's the bottom line here? This life-changing truth: Intolerance is *not* a dirty word. There are situations in which you *need* to be intolerant. Trust me, you don't want to bite into any rancid chicken! It's deadly! And wrong notions—no matter how popular or appealing they may be—are even more so.

THE **UNOFFICIAL**

5

LIFE IS SHORTER THAN YOU THINK

Show me, O LORD, my life's end and the
number of my days; let me know
how fleeting is my life.

PSALM 39:4

It used to be that death was pretty much an every-day fact of life: a barnyard cat savoring an unfortunate mouse one day, Dad slaughtering a hog the next. When a family member died—and that happened with great frequency—the funeral was usually held right there in the home. Friends and relatives came to view the body laid up in the living room. After a proper period of mourning, the dearly departed was buried right in the backyard.

Nowadays it's nothing like that. We've made death remote. Most of us don't have to kill our own food. When a loved one passes away, we commonly go to funeral homes. Burials occur in cemeteries that are generally off the beaten path. It seems as though we don't want to face death, and so we acknowledge it only grudgingly, and then, only in the margins of our lives.

My dad died of cancer my junior year of high school, and basically I remember a lot of casseroles and elderly people at our house. I recall how somber everyone was, but still the fact of death eluded me. I suspect, like 99 percent of all adolescents, I was suffering from the illusion of immortality. I viewed death as an aberration, something that, though it might happen to others, would surely never come looking for me.

This all changed the summer after my sophomore year of college. One afternoon I noticed a fat squirrel sitting on our birdfeeder feasting on a pile of sunflower seeds. Bored out of my mind, I picked up the air rifle used to ward off these unwelcome guests. Pumping it about fifteen times, I eased open the back door, aimed and squeezed. What happened next altered my life.

The pellet, rather than stinging the squirrel's hide and causing him to hightail it out of the backyard, pierced his gray fur. He fell over, bleeding and twitching. For about three minutes I watched him convulse, trying to hold on to his ebbing life. Then he became still. *Deathly* still.

I don't know why—as a kid I'd killed snakes and shot ducks on hunting trips—but something about killing this particular squirrel shook me. Like never before, the reality of death rocked me. That mysterious substance called life, whatever it was that had enabled the squirrel to run and climb and pick up a seed and nibble on it, was gone, never to return. For the first time, maybe ever, I began to think about my own eventual death. Later that summer, driving to Florida with friends late one night, we all—including the friend driving the car—fell asleep. We hurtled off the interstate at sixty miles an hour and flipped over.

THE **UNOFFICIAL**

Yet no one was even scratched! Another hundred yards and we would have gone off a bridge.

The point? Life is short and unpredictable. Your life is a "mist" (James 4:14), "grass" that quickly withers and dies (Ps. 90:5–6), a mere "breath" (Ps. 39:5). Like it or not, your days are numbered (Ps. 139:16), and each tick of the clock moves you closer to the appointed day when you will exit this life. It would be morbid for you to sit around and think about death all the time. But it would be foolish for you to go through life *never* thinking about death, and never getting ready for the life to come.

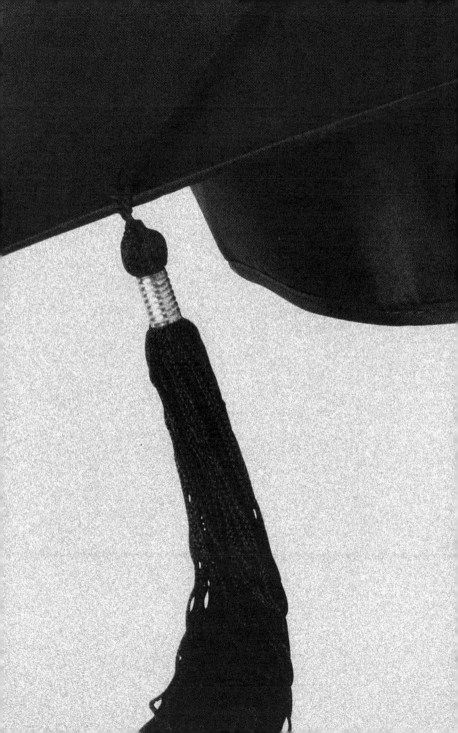

Truths
about
People

6

PEOPLE HAVE INFINITE WORTH

So God created man in his own image,
in the image of God he created him;
male and female he created them.

GENESIS 1:27

At a Shoney's restaurant far from campus, my roommate, several friends, and I were stuffing our faces. Somebody said something funny at the very instant I was swallowing a bite of salad. I chortled, choked, and snorted all at the same time, and—yes, it's gross but true—a piece of lettuce came flying out of my *nose!* Seeing that, my roommate also burst into laughter, spraying a mouthful of milk across the table. Years later, we still smile whenever we remember that moment.

On a sunny Saturday morning, twenty-five collegiates showed up to scrape and paint an old house in a bad neighborhood. The owner stood by with pride as his dingy brown home slowly but surely took on a sparkling white appearance. Nine hours later, the students retreated across the street to admire their finished work. They were exhausted and covered with paint. They had laughed and sweated. Each felt a strong sense of fulfillment.

At one level these are just common, everyday scenes of life after high school. At a deeper level, these ordinary moments proclaim an extraordinary truth: Humans bear the very image of God!

The image of God. Whatever in the world does that phrase mean? Centuries ago, theologians debated this mind-boggling concept at great length, writing thick tomes in Latin. *Imago Dei* is what they called it. But few people read theology texts—ancient or otherwise—anymore. And since most people have a limited knowledge of Latin, a clearer, more concise explanation is in order.

The image of God means that unlike all the other creatures on the planet, humans alone have an immortal soul that can connect both vertically with God and horizontally with other people. No other living thing has this capacity for deep and meaningful relationships on every level—emotional, mental, and spiritual.

The renowned author and Christian apologist C. S. Lewis put it this way in his classic address "The Weight of Glory":

> *There are no ordinary people. You have never talked to a mere mortal. Nations, cultures, arts, civilisations—these are mortal, and their life is to ours as the life of a gnat. But it is immortals whom we joke with, work with, marry, snub and exploit—immortal horrors or everlasting splendours.*

Lewis's words underscore what I am saying: Every person you meet today has infinite worth. Why? Because each was created *by* God *for* God. And so were you. But there's more.

The image of God also means that unlike plants and animals, we have the opportunity to make an eternal difference in the world. We have been given a divine mandate (and privilege!) to work with our Creator as he completes his vast plan for the universe (Ps. 8:3–8; Eph. 2:10). We show the life of Christ to neighbors and coworkers. We share the love of Christ with our family members and friends. We participate joyfully in the miracle of salvation. We struggle faithfully in the process of sanctification (i.e., the process of growing in our Christian faith). As we participate with the Lord in the building of his eternal kingdom, we are playing a crucial role in reclaiming for our God the honor and praise that he so richly deserves. Bearing his image, we reflect his glory!

People have infinite worth because they bear the image of God. Ask God to help you understand this reality in a life-changing way. Then do this experiment. For at least the next twenty-four hours, be especially observant. Look for hints of God's image in those around you. Identify ways in which our culture denies or ignores this great truth.

Once you truly grasp this concept, you can never feel insignificant again. And life, even in mundane places like restaurants and run-down neighborhoods, suddenly becomes quite magical and wonderful.

THE **UNOFFICIAL**

7

PEOPLE ARE NOT BASICALLY GOOD

It is not the explosive power of atomic war that I fear, but rather the explosive power for evil in the hearts of men.

ALBERT EINSTEIN

My friend Bill was in my dorm room, messing around. I don't recall exactly what he was doing or why I was in such a foul humor. I just remember that Bill was getting on my nerves big time.

As I stood there tossing darts, Bill continued to annoy and irritate me. My mood degenerated further. Finally, Bill said or did something, and I just snapped. Wheeling around without warning, my eyes flashing, I reared back and fired a dart straight at Bill!

He tried to lunge out of the way, but in a twelve-by-twelve-foot dorm room, it's hard to miss or be missed. The dart struck him solidly in the upper thigh near his hip.

He yelped, and then became very quiet. Instantly, I was filled with horror at what I had done. I began to issue apologies left and right. I offered Band-Aids, help, food, the use of my car, my firstborn male child—anything he wanted. In shock, he handed me the dart, and with a nervous look on his face that said, "Len, you are a certified psycho!" he smiled weakly and mumbled something about needing to study.

As he shut the door behind him, I was left sitting on my bed to ponder the gravity of and the reason for my sudden, violent display.

Why are we this way? To be sure, most people have never used a friend for a dartboard, but we *all* are guilty of wrong acts. Why do toddlers, without the first lesson in deception, naturally lie? Why do grade school kids gang up on those who are weaker? Why do we cheat, steal, gossip, get jealous, and use people for selfish ends? Why do we cruise through life largely indifferent to the needs of others and primarily obsessed with figuring out how to get what we want?

Theologians explain our tendency toward evil by using the word *depravity*. A translation of the Greek term *adokimos,* it means literally "not standing the test." That is to say, we fail the test of pleasing God. Why? Because he is perfect, and we are morally corrupt. Our souls are crooked, our wills—that part of us that makes choices—are rebellious and perverted (Rom. 1:28–31; 2 Peter 2:19).

According to the Bible, we're not sinners because we sin; rather, we sin because we're sinners. In other words, our depravity is a condition we're born with. It's inherited. When Adam and Eve sinned, human nature itself underwent a radical change. Consequently, when Adam and Eve had children, they passed this tendency toward sin on to their offspring. Whether you call it inherited sin, original sin, or a sin nature, the fact is we all have an innate "dark side."

Now this doesn't mean we're each destined to turn out like Adolf Hitler or Jeffrey Dahmer. Nor does it mean that humans are incapable of doing some good and positive things. There is still something beautiful and occasionally noble within the human soul, if only because we are created in the image of God (see chap. 6). However, measured against a holy God, we all fall woefully short. In our depraved state, sin is the natural and normal outcome. We should not be surprised when people do evil. Why? Because humans are *not* basically good.

Granted, this is not a popular teaching. Our culture, enamored with Eastern thought and the human potential movement, has embraced the opposite notion. And why not? Which message sounds better to you?

a. *"You are magnificent, and your greatest need is to get in touch with the divine spark within you"* (New Age thought).
b. *"You are sinful, depraved, and spiritually dead, and your biggest problem is that you need to turn from your evil ways and turn humbly to a holy God for forgiveness and life"* (biblical Christianity).

This explains why human depravity is a truth that most people simply refuse to accept. "What do you mean I'm *not* basically good? How dare you insult me!" It's offensive to think something is inherently wrong with us. How much easier to blame our problems on someone else or on our surroundings. How much less threatening to spend all our money and to focus all our energy on massive efforts to try to improve society. And yet for all our stunning scientific achievements, our bold new social programs, and our innovative educational advances, you'd have to agree our culture is more corrupt than ever before. Why? Because society cannot change until individual hearts change.

Bertrand Russell, the agnostic mathematician and philosopher, said it well: "Man still has a caveman's heart. We must find a way to change the caveman's heart."

What's the solution for our "caveman's heart," that is, our depravity? Is humanity doomed to be a race of people who throw darts at each other—or worse? What do I tell my four-year-old son when he flagrantly disobeys, I discipline him, and he laments, "I don't know *how* to be good!"?

Here's what the Bible says. When sinners face up to their depravity, and when they trust in Jesus Christ to pardon all their sins, God performs supernatural surgery on their souls. He deals a death blow to their old sinful nature (Rom. 6:6; Gal. 5:24), and he gives them a new nature and identity, the very life of Christ dwelling within (2 Cor. 5:17; Gal. 2:20). Not only that, but God also implants his Spirit within them (1 Cor. 12:13). As they yield control of their lives to the indwelling Spirit of God, they find the power to say no to that old sinful nature (Gal. 5:16–25).

That's the only hope I know of for depraved, dart-throwing people. Though we are not good, God is . . . good enough and big enough to change us from the inside out.

8

NOBODY HAS IT TOGETHER

We're all pitiful people.

MARY OWEN

Terri was not only a popular sorority girl but also an LSU cheerleader. With her Christian faith, sweet personality, gorgeous tan, and dazzling smile, she was a "catch." And guess what? She was *my* girlfriend.

I know, I know . . . you're thinking, "If this guy expects me to buy *this* story, he's in La-La Land." Hey, look, I can't explain it either. The whole thing is one of life's great puzzles. My only theory is that there *must* be some truth to the old saying, "Love is blind."

I remember once being at a party with Terri. As I looked around at all the beautiful people—girls with flawless figures, guys with massive physiques, all impeccably dressed, each so polished—I suddenly felt very insecure.

You'll never believe what I did . . . or maybe you will. I took my skinny self to the rest room, locked the door, and began doing push-ups! Why? I don't know for sure. I guess I thought I could make my arms and chest look bigger with a few seconds of intense exercise.

Can you picture this whole scene in your head? In the living room you've got all these apparently confident people smiling and joking and looking so "together." In the bathroom down the hall you've got a scrawny guy grunting and puffing while he bobs up and down next to the toilet.

It's a pathetic picture, I know. Why am I willing to share such an embarrassing story? Because I believe it emphasizes a universal truth. We're all insecure. And despite appearances, none of us has it together. In the words of my wife's Aunt Mary, "We're all pitiful people." That's not meant as a slam or an insult. Just a statement of fact. Let me explain.

For most of the last twenty years, I have been involved with students in the sixteen- to twenty-four-year-old age bracket. During that time, I've met some very blessed individuals. Some of them certified geniuses. Some stunningly attractive. Some from wealthy families. Some fantastic athletes. Some immensely popular.

And what I've discovered, once you get beneath the surface, is that we *all* wrestle with our own personal demons. No matter how good-looking, gifted, or funny we may be, we all fear rejection. We all want desperately to be accepted. We all go into the bathroom, if not to do push-ups, at least to stare at our reflection in the mirror and ask ourselves haunting questions.

"When people see me, what is it they see? And do they *like* what they see? How can I hide my flaws—my big nose, my broad hips, my shameful past, my enormous fear of rejection? How can I project an image of togetherness? I want people to admire my looks, my accomplishments, my reputation, my personality, my spirituality," which, if you think about it, translates into, "I can't be overweight, or ever fail, or reveal my past, or be in a bad mood, or express doubts about God."

What is the inevitable result of this intense pressure to have it all together? We wear masks. We put on an act. We pretend. We live a lie. Because we know in our hearts we're not at all what we pretend to be, we feel like impostors. And since we often foolishly believe the lie that others really *are* what they appear to be, we feel like colossal failures. The end result of all this is exhaustion and frustration.

I want to propose a better way. It's the way of realization and truth. It's the way of humility and honesty. It involves getting over the illusion that you or I or anyone else in this world has it together.

We simply don't. We're flawed and quirky and strange creatures. How wonderfully freeing it is finally to be able to say, "I am who I am. I am in the truest sense of the word a pitiful person. I'm insecure. I'm the kind of guy who feels tempted to do push-ups in the bathroom to win acceptance. But no longer am I going to pretend to be something I'm not. Nor am I going to be intimidated by people who seem to have a picture-perfect life. Even if I can't see it, those individuals struggle with real problems too."

I've discovered something else. When we're honest about who we are, lots of good things happen. By admitting I don't have it together, I've found a far deeper appreciation of God's love. He accepts me unconditionally, just as I am. I've gained friends who were warmed and helped by my openness. I like to think I've helped some of them find the courage to put aside some of their own masks. And I've found life as a whole to be much more enjoyable. I feel alive and authentic, genuinely glad to be who God made me.

A short P.S. to the story above. Terri and I eventually went our separate ways. A lucky guy scooped her up. Then about five years later God brought a gorgeous woman named Cindi into my life. How fun it is to be a pitiful person married to another pitiful person and to be crazy about one another, despite all the flaws and imperfections. Wow!

I wish that for you.

9

NOBODY GETS AWAY WITH ANYTHING

Everybody, sooner or later, sits down to a banquet of consequences.
ROBERT L. STEVENSON

I'll never forget the day at LSU when a friend loaned me his moped. I found a cute girl and we tooled all over the place—past the lakes, down sorority row, through the quad.

As the sun went down, the night turned cool and homework beckoned. I dropped off my date and began buzzing home. Several blocks from my house, as I came to a red light, a thought flew into my head: *If I were on a bike, I wouldn't stop, and this moped is really nothing more than a motorized bike.*

So I slowed down just enough to make sure no cars were coming and then zipped right through the intersection . . . only to notice a pair of headlights coming down the other side of the boulevard. *Wouldn't it be my luck if that were a cop?* A second or two passed, and then the approaching headlights were joined by flashing blue lights!

To this day I still don't know why I panicked, but I did. Realizing I was a mere four blocks from my street, I thought, *I can outrun him!* Giving the little yellow moped full throttle, I ducked low in an attempt to become aerodynamic.

For a moment, I thought my plan was working, but when I looked back I saw my pursuer was already to a place where he could make a U-turn. He was gaining on me fast! I had to go to plan B. *Since I can't outrun him, I'll start making turns!* I took the next right, killed the lights and engine, and coasted into a dark driveway. Getting behind an old pickup truck, I lay down. Immediately, a blur of flashing blue lights went streaking past the driveway and around the curve in the road.

I considered running—until I realized I couldn't just leave my buddy's scooter there. So I began looking for a gate into an alley or another yard. *I'll wait here all night if I have to. I'll . . .*

My frantic thoughts were stilled (and my heart too!) when I saw the police car come back and stop directly in front of the driveway in which I was hiding. The door creaked open. I watched a burly man step out of the car. He flicked on a flashlight and began coming up the drive.

I had thought I was so slick. I had been sure I could get away with running a red light. With my "speedy" moped and "superior" smarts, I didn't make it two blocks or two minutes!

My moped incident was an awfully humbling experience, but it taught me a great lesson. Wrong choices *always* have bad consequences—often short-term, but definitely long-term. It's just a fact: Nobody gets away with anything. There is a payday someday. Even if we seem to skate through this life, we all have to face a day of accounting in the next. God takes note of everything we do. Unbelievers will face the "great white throne judgment" (Rev. 20:11–15), and believers will stand before the "judgment seat of Christ" (2 Cor. 5:10). The Bible says it well, "Do not be deceived: God cannot be mocked. A man reaps what he sows" (Gal. 6:7).

Take it from me . . . it's no fun to stand before a judge when you know and he knows you're guilty. And now that I think about it, I'm not so sure mopeds are all that fun either.

THE **UNOFFICIAL**

10

PEOPLE WERE CREATED FOR RELATIONSHIPS

Ah, look at all the lonely people!
THE BEATLES, "ELEANOR RIGBY"

Fast forward your life ten years. You're finished (or almost finished) with college, grad school, law school, or med school. Or you've completed your hitch in the armed forces. Perhaps you've settled into a career. Maybe you're married and have a couple kids. What is it you'll remember most about your life during those ten years?

I doubt you'll be thinking of that lecture you once heard on the endocrine system. Nor will you recall much about that one-day seminar you attended on inventory management. What you *will* remember are the people from your life. You will laugh about old roommates and bad blind dates. You may think of crusty old Professor Dipstick (even if you can't recall a single lecture he ever gave). You will wonder about former flames. You will reminisce about dorm neighbors or fellow employees from days gone by.

Why are we this way? Why do almost all our memories—good and bad—revolve around people? The answer lies in the very nature of God. Orthodox Christianity teaches that though God is one, he exists eternally in three persons—Father, Son, and Holy Spirit—who live in perfect relationship with each other.

Thus, to be created in the image of God means that we too are meant to live in relationship. We are designed to love, serve, interact, listen, give, submit, encourage, share, cooperate, confront, hug, sympathize, and so on, and to receive those things in return.

But by the time we get through high school, most of us have learned that relating to others is hard and involves serious risks. Relationships often feature the sting of rejection. People are capable of inflicting horrendous pain. A single rude comment about my physique during a tenth grade high school drafting class has never left my mind.

Over time, such negative experiences cause us to be wary and guarded. We erect thick, protective walls around our hearts. We develop the art of superficiality. I realized some years ago that I have a tendency to use humor as a way to keep conversations and situations from becoming too personal. By making a joke out of everything, I am able to keep people at arm's length. Others learn to stay busy and safe by throwing themselves into tasks and projects that don't involve interacting with others on a deep level. The consequences of such "relational reluctance" are severe. I'm convinced, if we could administer truth serum to the entire adult population, the overwhelming majority would admit they feel isolated and lonely. They desperately want deep relationships with others, because that's how they were created, but they're scared to death to pursue them!

What does all this have to do with you? Simply this: The whole world lies before you. You have the opportunity to do almost anything. But in the next few years, if you neglect the pursuit of deep relationships with others, including God, you will miss out on *the* greatest blessing of life.

THE **UNOFFICIAL**

I found an old journal of mine from my college days. One entry, written following a breakup, says it well: "Why continue to love when it invariably ends up hurting so incredibly? . . . Not to love is to die, to do so brings the same results. . . . Inside, I know there is a point and I know it is the only way to live. And yet the same, aching soul asks, 'What's the use?'

"Meanwhile God prepares me for another go at it somewhere, sometime. And you know what? I'd be an idiot *not* to go for it on an even grander scale. Taking risks is the only way to live."

Hey, though it's scary and risky, the fact is you were built to enjoy deep relationships. That's the path to fulfillment in this life (Eccles. 4:9–12). The question is will you go for it?

Truths
about
You

YOU DON'T KNOW EVERYTHING

I not only use all the brains I have,
but all I can borrow.

WOODROW WILSON

My senior year of high school (back near the end of the Mesozoic era), you could have summarized our class mood in these words: "Look, we've endured thirteen years of formal schooling (fourteen, if you count preschool). We know enough to stand on our own and make our own decisions. Therefore, we don't need or want any unsolicited advice or help. Please leave us alone!"

I'm guessing you have these feelings too. You've got a full-blown case of senioritis. You want to spread your wings, move out there into the adult world, and get on with your life. Isn't that what they've been telling you commencement means— the beginning of the rest of your life? My bet is you're getting sick of all the Hallmark sentiments and tips for success. You just want to fly the coop and be free, make your own decisions, be grown-up, and be treated like a grown-up.

I want that for you too. The fact is you're entering an exciting, occasionally scary, and certainly critical phase of life. In the next four to six years, it's probable you'll make one or more of the three biggest decisions we all face:

1. *Who or what will be my master?*
2. *What will be my mission in life?*
3. *Who will be my mate?*

Now, I know the last thing you want is advice. So I won't preach at you or try to give you career tips. But I do want to remind you of a wise truth: You don't know everything.

That's not meant as an insult. Your generation might very well be the most knowledgeable generation in history. No, that statement (an undeniable fact, actually) is intended simply to warn you against foolish pride. You are not as cosmopolitan as you may think, or at least not as worldly wise as many of the people you will encounter.

Despite all your life experiences and education, you're going to bump up against some intensely confusing situations in the next few years. Believe it or not, you're going to meet people who have been around the block a few more times than you. Remember your elementary school playground? How the bigger, older kids often took advantage of the younger, more naive children? That's the dynamic you're facing now, only on an adult scale. And the consequences from here on out are much more painful than a scraped knee resulting from a shove off the monkey bars.

So . . . because it is, as they say, a dog-eat-dog world, because it does get harsh out there, because you don't know everything—though you may indeed know a lot—you need some older and wiser mentors for this next stage of the journey. You need people you respect whom you can ask for help and advice.

Your mentor might prove to be a campus minister, a Christian professor, or an

older fraternity brother or sorority sister who is a solid believer in Jesus. Your source of counsel might come from a married couple in your church or from a dorm Bible study group.

I don't know exactly where you'll find godly guidance. I just hope you will make it a priority to look for someone who's a bit further down the road. I trust you won't be arrogant like so many of my high school friends were. In their pride they refused to solicit advice. They knew what was best . . . or so they foolishly thought. With that mind-set, a number of them made decisions that haunt them to this day. I know this for a fact because I saw some of them recently at a high school reunion.

Somehow or another, in our do-it-yourself culture, we've bought into the idea that asking for help is a sign of weakness. It's not. It's a mark of great humility and uncommon wisdom.

You don't know everything. And guess what? I don't either. But if we at least know we need others to help us through—and we always will—we'll stay far ahead of the pack.

12

YOU CAN MEASURE YOUR SPIRITUAL MATURITY BY HOW WELL YOU LOVE

And if I have the gift of prophecy,
and know all mysteries and all knowledge;
and if I have all faith, so as to remove
mountains, but do not have love,
I am nothing.

1 CORINTHIANS 13:2 NASB

The first semester of my freshman year at LSU, I was the victim of a divine ambush.

I went to a Campus Crusade for Christ fall retreat for one primary reason: to meet girls. I don't know if that happened or not. I *do* remember encountering God in a life-changing way. I remember a Saturday morning session in an open air pavilion with concrete floors and benches. I remember a speaker named Dan Hayes. I remember being mesmerized as he explained that the Christian life is a moment-by-moment relationship with Jesus, not a once-a-week religious exercise. Dan described what it means to allow Jesus to be the Lord of every aspect of our lives. He explained how to walk in the power of God's Spirit. As he concluded, all I could think was, *This is what I've been missing. This is what I need to do, what I want to do. More than anything else in the whole world, I want to know Christ deeply and walk with him.* It was a holy and miraculous moment, I'm sure, because sitting there surrounded by dozens of girls, my thoughts were solely on God. He was my heart's desire.

Afterwards, an older and wiser friend walked with me out into a giant field. We sat down and he answered my many questions. Then we prayed together, and something profound happened, something I still find difficult to express in words. I felt, to borrow the words of John Wesley, "my heart strangely warmed." Though I had been a Christian since I was ten or twelve, I still look back on this mysterious experience as a college freshman as the turning point in my spiritual journey.

In the following days, I learned that in the same way we grow physically, we are expected to mature spiritually (Eph. 4:13–15). This process of spiritual growth and life change (theologians refer to it as sanctification) became my obsession. How do I get to know Christ better? How do I become more like him? How do I live under his control?

I suppose it would be fair to say that these questions have haunted my life for the last twenty plus years. And during this same time I've learned that different Christians have different ideas about what constitutes spiritual maturity.

I've met people who regard mastery of the Bible as "proof" that a person is mature. Person A can quote the book of Galatians from memory, therefore, she must be extremely godly. Person B knows Galatians in Greek; he is a certified spiritual giant! Others equate theological insight with "evidence" of spiritual sophistication. Since Bob can articulate all the ins and outs of Reformed theology, he must be a solid, committed Christian.

For some, it all comes down to various experiences. If you speak in tongues or are slain in the Spirit, you are regarded as spiritual. For others, maturity is measured by externals such as attending Christian activities, wearing Christian T-shirts, using Christian lingo, or attending Christian concerts. The more "Christian" things you do, say, or wear, the reasoning goes, the more spiritual you are.

I guess there are almost as many understandings of what spiritual maturity looks like as there are believers in Jesus. But most of these are inadequate barometers. Consider: If Bible knowledge alone makes one "mature," then how do we explain the "Scripture scholar" who is a jerk to her friends or the "theological genius" who is downright mean to his waitress? If having an emotional experience is proof of godliness, then what's with the Sunday holy roller who turns into a Friday night Cain raiser? If Christian involvement is all that is required for spirituality, what do we do with that "active" believer in her rapture T-shirt who refuses to speak to her roommate?

The truth is sanctification can't be measured by superficial standards. Maturity is not a simplistic process. It isn't formulaic. It doesn't boil down to "If you just do/learn/experience/wear_____, then presto—you are mature."

No, according to Jesus (Mark 12:28–31; John 13:34–35), the apostle Paul (1 Corinthians 13), and the apostle John (1 John 4:7–21), *love* is the distinguishing mark of maturity. It's the ultimate measuring stick. Not love for "cute chicks or hunky guys"—anyone can feel that—but God's otherworldly, unconditional love. Forgiving love for grouchy professors and imperfect parents. Sacrificial love for those who can and will never pay you back. Risky love for those who may very well *stab* you in the back! Courageous love that boldly— yet tenderly—urges wayward brothers and sisters to come back home.

So how do we do it? How do we become loving Christians? That's the age-old question. We want five simple steps to follow or a glorious one-time experience in church that will forever transform us. But there is no such solution. There are no shortcuts to maturity.

Maturity is a lifelong, violent wrestling match between the natural desire to be selfish and the God-given desire to care for others. It is brutal. It is agonizing. It is not for the squeamish.

You want to be mature? You will have to let go of your superficial "Christian" illusions and look painfully at your own sinful heart. You will have to trust deeply in the goodness of God. You will have to rely on supernatural strength. You will have to move out of your comfort zone.

You need to know you will end up bruised and bloodied by the demands and risks of love. Even in victory, you may end up looking like a loser. But if you go the distance, despite your wounds, you will be fully alive (2 Cor. 4:7–15; 6:3–13). And rather than merely impressing people with your Bible knowledge, you will, to paraphrase the words of Larry Crabb, be seductive, enticing others to pursue the God you have come to know so well.

That's a lot to lay on you, I know. But it's a truth I began to discover that gorgeous fall weekend in 1976. And it's a truth I'm still trying to grasp and live out today.

13

YOU NEED THE CHURCH ALMOST AS MUCH AS THE CHURCH NEEDS YOU

And let us consider how we may spur one another on toward love and good deeds. Let us not give up meeting together, as some are in the habit of doing, but let us encourage one another—and all the more as you see the Day approaching.

HEBREWS 10:24–25

With more than twenty-five thousand students, LSU was larger than my hometown. I remember being stunned that first week of college as it dawned on me that the campus was a veritable city within a city. Traffic was terrible—a perpetual rush hour. Activity was nonstop. From the air, the place surely must have resembled a stirred-up ant pile. The university never stopped or rested . . . until Sunday morning came along.

I woke up on my first Lord's Day as a collegiate to a silence that was almost deafening. The campus had a tranquil, almost surrealistic feel. I noted with fascination that parking lots remained full and still, until about 1:00 P.M. Then throughout the remainder of the afternoon, this "ghost town" slowly hummed to life. This was the weekly procedure my four years there.

Though I was not studying to be a rocket scientist (and I confess I never even took a course in that major), I quickly realized a universal truth: The majority of young adults stop attending church when they graduate from high school. Church involvement is neither a priority nor a part of their weekly routine.

Perhaps this is your plan as well. If you've been prodded and/or coerced by parents to attend weekly worship services, it may well be that you plan to discontinue this practice once you move away from home, especially if you've been raised in a church that seems out of touch with real life (and there are plenty of those).

As a college freshman, I experienced this same lack of enthusiasm for organized religion. Growing up, I suppose I had, by most standards, a pretty decent church experience. Still, I had been forced to sit through my share of bad sermons. I'd endured plenty of hokey music performed badly by well-meaning, would-be soloists. I'd run into countless hypocrites. There were times when I had questioned the legitimacy of church altogether. I had posed the questions we all inevitably ask: Why do I have to get up on Sundays and dress up to go to a special building to worship God? Isn't God everywhere? Besides, I get together with Christian friends all the time! Doesn't that count for something?

Now that I think about it, I recall spending more than a few Sunday mornings at college in a horizontal position, "worshiping" at what my friends and I jokingly used to call "Bedside Baptist" or "The Church of the Inner Springs."

All these years later, I am even more aware of the faults and foibles of churches. Not long ago, I attended the services at a student's hometown church, and—I don't know how else to say it—the experience was absolutely terrible! The service was endless, pointless, irrelevant, and dull. I remember thinking, *No wonder so many students abandon church! What a waste! A person could find more inspiration and excitement reading the local phone book!*

I'm sensitive to this kind of stuff, because now, you see, I work on a church staff. For the last eight years, I've spent my waking hours planning worship services, preparing sermons, leading small groups, organizing retreats, teaching Bible studies—all in an ongoing attempt to say to collegiates, "Don't give up on church! God *is* real and big and exciting—even though local churches often obscure him with goofy and outdated programs. God *is* in the business of changing lives—even though many congregations often spend their time squabbling over ridiculous issues like what color the choir robes should be."

Believe me, I've seen the dark side of church. I've seen how petty Christians can be, how hateful some act in the name of God. I've been embarrassed by the antics of certain TV preachers. There have been times when I wanted to throw up my hands and walk away in disgust. I've heard—and identified with—the common wisecracks about church:

- *"Christians have done the one thing to Christianity and Christ that even Christ's enemies couldn't do. . . . We have made Him boring"* (Dan Hayes).
- *"The church is like Noah's ark. If it wasn't for the storm on the outside, we wouldn't be able to stand the stench on the inside."*
- *"God's three great humiliations are Christ's taking on human flesh, Christ's taking on the sins of the world, and the church"* (Dorothy Sayers).

And yet in spite of all these facts, I still believe in the church. It is the one institution on the face of the earth that Jesus promised to bless and build (Matt. 16:18). For all its flaws, my local congregation is occasionally a glorious place. We try to preach the truth with integrity and creativity and relevance. We work at building true community between believers. And every now and then, despite ourselves, we somehow manage to catch a glimpse of what heaven will be like.

It's for these reasons I urge my collegiates not just to attend Sunday morning services but to plug in to the very life of the church. I try to hook students up with families. I encourage them to get involved in hands-on ministry to kids and junior highers. I want to see them passing out the communion elements, serving on workdays, singing with the worship team.

The ones who do this—who choose to look past all the church's imperfections and become actively involved—reap some huge benefits: They find lifetime friendships with older, wiser Christians. They discover marital and parenting role models. They gain homes away from home where they can do a load of laundry or enjoy a real meal. They find fulfillment as they use their God-given abilities in serving others, as they energize lifeless congregations. They prepare for "the real world" after college, where there are plenty of churches but no campus ministries. And most of all, they realize they have a huge and valuable contribution to make to the building of Christ's kingdom.

It's not a major sin to visit "Bedside Baptist" every now and then, but it would be a tragedy if you chose to "join" that small and insignificant congregation. Please don't make that mistake. You *do* need the church, and, speaking as an insider, let me say, the church desperately needs you.

14

YOU WILL BE EITHER A CHRISTIAN WHO CONSUMES OR A CHRISTIAN WHO COMMITS

The fear of commitment is epidemic in the Western world.

JERRY WHITE

Accompany college sophomores Jeff and Stephanie on a shopping expedition. Their goal is simple: find new clothes for homecoming weekend. They park at the west end of Northbrook Mall, scurry through the brisk October air, and enter the friendly confines of a large department store.

How pleasant it is! Warm (but not too warm), soothing music playing softly in the background, everything impeccably clean, an abundance of wares tastefully displayed. It is a veritable feast for the senses. None of this is by accident. Marketers and researchers have been studying consumer preferences for years. Everything—from the intensity of the lighting to the colors of the store's flooring—has been carefully chosen so as to put customers in the optimal buying mood.

Ah, but Jeff and Stephanie are sophisticated and savvy. They don't just grab the first thing they see. They are skeptical. They have to be convinced. "Is this product well made?" "Can I get the same item somewhere else for a lower price?"

Therein lies the beauty of the mall. Each merchant competes with the rest. Loaded with cash (or at least plastic), shoppers are at the center of the mall universe. Everything revolves around the consumer! It's a colossal contest to see which store can woo, please, pamper, and keep the most customers.

Ultimately, the merchant who gets Jeff and Stephanie's patronage is the one who gives them the best deal. "I want quality, and I want it at the lowest cost imaginable. Serve me, give me exactly what I want, don't offend me, and don't dare ask me to pay much." The store that is able to pull off that difficult task is the store that gets the most business.

But such "loyalty" is very fickle. One slipup—a defective product, a sales clerk having a bad day, inconvenient hours—and most shoppers just take their business elsewhere. There's another store right next door that will gladly try to accommodate, and one next to that, and one next to that . . .

What's the point of this analogy? Simply this: When it comes to church membership or involvement in campus Christian organizations, many high school graduates display little or no commitment. On the contrary, they function as consumers. They view various Christian groups as "stores" in a kind of "spiritual mall." In a very real way, these religious entities are seen as competing with one another to see who can offer the slickest program, the most helpful ministry. And so many Christians "shop" around.

This is a common phenomenon on college campuses. Many students float all over the religious map—the Baptist Student Union on Mondays, Campus Crusade on Tuesdays, Inter-Varsity meetings on Wednesdays, Chi Alpha on Thursdays, a different church each Sunday. And while it is wise for freshmen to check out the various religious groups before they decide where to get involved, it is *not* healthy for students to continue this kind of noncommittal behavior indefinitely. Yet many do. They never land anywhere. They never plug in. They want to be part of every group and do everything, and in trying to have it all, they end up with very little. That's the deception inherent in "consumer Christianity." By always asking, "What's in this for me?" students might experience a fun meeting one night with one group, or a great retreat the following weekend with students from another ministry, but they never find the deeper joy of serving, of giving themselves and investing their time and talents to make a difference, of developing deep relationships.

Unless something radical happens, these individuals will continue to go through life as consumer Christians. When they find a church that is pleasing to them, that makes them feel good, they will patronize it, if not with their effort and money, at least with their presence. All will be well until that church slips up. As soon as these uncommitted consumers don't get anything out of the music or the sermons, they will take their business to the congregation down the street. If that new group ever asks them to pay a high price—whether spiritual, emotional, or financial—our shopper friends will be on the move again. When their next church offends, a common experience when Christians speak the truth in love, they will again leave to find a church that will only tell them what they want to hear. The minute that church has struggles, the spiritual shoppers in its midst will be quick to criticize rather than quick to lend a hand.

The students I know with the best college experiences are those who checked out an assortment of groups and local churches. They prayed about where to get involved, then they jumped in. They used their gifts and abilities to serve. They let others know them up close, see their faults, and help them change. They saw themselves, not as passive consumers but as active ministers. When their groups struggled, they didn't bail out and start looking for another more successful ministry to join. They renewed their commitment, joined together with their fellow members, and worked to make things better.

Consider this a challenge to reject the snare of consumer Christianity. Realize you can't do everything. You can't join every Christian group and be friends with every believer on campus. Such a lifestyle leads to a superficial and inconsequential Christian experience—a mile wide but only an inch deep.

THE UNOFFICIAL

15

YOU DON'T
HAVE TO SIN

The question asked by more people since the beginning of time is "Why do I keep doing this stuff to myself?"

JAMES T. EVANS

Recently I caught a snake near our house. With two small, very curious, very fearless sons, and with evidence suggesting I just might have a deadly cottonmouth on my hands, I realized there was only one course of action to take. I got a shovel and, with one hard thrust, beheaded the serpent. The creature convulsed briefly then became still. Ten minutes later, when I attempted to pick up the body parts to dispose of them, the head suddenly jerked, its jaws opening wide as if to strike at me. For another twenty or thirty minutes, every time I poked the severed head, I got the same reaction. Of course my boys thought this was the coolest thing ever.

Reflecting on the snake's behavior later on, I was reminded of a profound spiritual truth: Christians don't *have* to sin.

Now you're wondering, "How did this guy go from a dead snake in his front lawn to a theological truth about sin?" Let me explain. According to the

New Testament, when we put our faith in Jesus, we were joined to him. How? The Spirit of God "baptized" us into the body of Christ (1 Cor. 12:13). This union or association with Jesus means a lot of things, but one of the most mind-boggling truths is this: We were somehow spiritually present with Christ when he was crucified (Rom. 6:1–14). The cross, then, was not only a place where Jesus died for our sins, but it also served as God's "cosmic shovel" to strike a death blow at that part of *us* that loves to sin. In a very real yet hard-to-grasp way, our old sinful nature was "beheaded." It no longer has real power over us, because it no longer is alive.

In its place, God has planted a new nature—the very life of Christ (Gal. 2:20). Because we are brand-new people (2 Cor. 5:17) and the Spirit of God lives in us (Rom. 8:9), we truly have the power to resist sin and pursue righteousness (Gal. 5:16–25).

If all this is true, you ask, why do we still sin? Well, like the lifeless snake that kept "fighting," our crucified sinful nature refuses to surrender easily. Even in death it continues to kick and scream. It *seems* alive. And when we get in certain situations where, for whatever reason, we forget what's really true about us, those old dead reflexes and sinful habits kick in. Suddenly we're doing things that go totally against who we really are as new creatures in Christ.

Think about it. You don't *have* to sin! As you prepare to launch out into life, into a whole new world of adult temptations, it's imperative that you make this life-changing truth your own.

To realize this truth more and more in your life . . .

- *You will need the constant help and encouragement of other Christians who can keep you on track.*
- *You will have to cling to God's promise of "resistible" temptations (1 Cor. 10:13). God has pledged that you will never be tempted beyond your ability to endure. [Note: The more you resist the tempting appeals of the old nature, the easier it becomes to resist. But the converse is also true. The more you yield to sin's urges, the easier it will be to give in next time!]*
- *You will have to develop a consuming passion for Jesus Christ. The easiest time to say no to sin is when you are saying a deep yes to Christ.*

A long time ago, a deadly serpent helped bring sin into the world (Genesis 3). My hope is that the dead snake I've told you about here can serve to remind you that sin doesn't have to be part of *your* life.

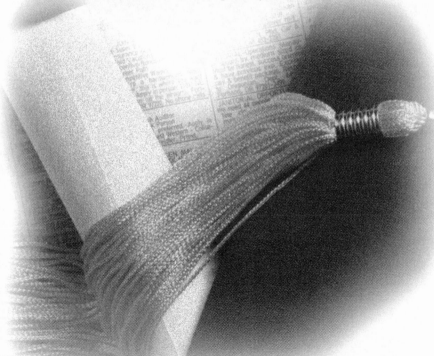

Truths
about
God

16

GOD IS GOOD

Now the serpent . . . said to the woman,
"Did God really say, 'You must not eat
from any tree in the garden'?"
GENESIS 3:1, EMPHASIS ADDED

As a college pastor, it's my job to introduce students to Christ and then help them develop a rich and authentic relationship with him. This means spending time with students and getting to know them. This, in turn, requires that I play lots of racquetball, hoops, and golf and that I frequently eat with them at the all-you-can-eat pizza buffet near campus. (Yep, it's a tough job, but somebody's got to do it!)

College ministry is not all fun and games, however. The stories students tell me are often heartbreaking—homes shattered by divorce, histories of immorality and guilt, secret struggles with addictive behaviors. One girl involved in our group lost both parents in a car wreck her senior year of high school. Then, less than one year later, her only sister was killed in another automobile accident!

The details vary, but the hurts are real for us all. And because of the pain we've endured, our great struggle in life is believing that God is good.

What do we mean by the goodness of God? A. W. Tozer, a writer from another era, said that "the goodness of God is that which disposes Him to be kind, cordial, benevolent, and full of good will toward men. . . . By His nature He is inclined to bestow blessedness and He takes holy pleasure in the happiness of His people" (*The Knowledge of the Holy,* 82).

That's a mouthful, but focus just on that last phrase. God "takes holy pleasure in the happiness of His people." In other words, he wants the absolute best for you and me. He is delighted when we are deeply fulfilled.

Why is this idea so hard for us to believe? Because we live in a fallen world full of pain where we have an enemy (i.e., Satan) who from the beginning has implied that God is unreasonable and harsh (Genesis 3). By camping out at the hard or confusing junctures of life, the devil craftily "reinterprets" God and events, planting seeds of doubt about God's intentions, suggesting that he is withholding something good from us. No wonder Scripture calls Satan the father of lies (John 8:44)!

Buying into the lies of Satan has serious consequences. If I am not convinced God is good, I certainly won't trust him. And if I don't trust him, there's no way I'm going to obey his commands! In short, the belief that God is good is foundational to right living.

Yet, how do we reconcile God's goodness with the pain all about us? Our goal here is not to give a comprehensive explanation for why God allows suffering. But consider this truth: A person can *be* good and have good purposes even while doing things or allowing things that don't *seem* good. For instance . . .

- Pain and discomfort can serve a good purpose. *A tetanus shot hurts like you know what, but not nearly as much as the disease it prevents. Working out can be excruciating, but consider the long-term benefits. What is it athletes often say? "No pain, no gain."*
- Discipline, though unpleasant, is good. *Negative consequences can teach us to make positive and right choices in the future.*

- Not getting what we want is often good. *Does my seven-year-old think my refusal to buy him a BB gun is "good"? No way! But it is! Having a dangerous weapon now would be detrimental to him (not to mention to our car windows) in ways he doesn't have the wisdom or experience to anticipate.*
- Being free to venture out into a fallen world where bad things can—and will—happen is good. *If you think about it, God could eliminate most bad things from our lives simply by keeping us locked up in padded rooms. If we were never allowed to drive, swim, interact with others, eat pizza, and so on, it's fairly certain we would never have a wreck, drown, catch an infectious disease, or choke on mozzarella cheese. The more restrictions, the better our chance of safety. But who wants to live like that? Freedom, even with all its risks, is far more preferable.*

How then can we know God's goodness in more than a theoretical way? First we need to reflect deeply and often on the events of Good Friday. Don't you think that's an odd and ironic label? If anything, it was Grim Friday, Ghastly Friday, Gruesome Friday. And then Sad, Sickening Saturday . . . until Mary came on Sunday morning with the news of the risen Christ. The events that happened that first Easter weekend show the lengths our good God is willing to go to eradicate evil and to insure our ultimate happiness. Though we still go through painful—sometimes awful—experiences, the cross demonstrates, in the words of Frederick Buechner, "there is no evil so dark and so obscene—not even this—but that God can turn it to good" (*Wishful Thinking,* 24).

Second, we need to experience God, and put him to the test. C. S. Lewis said: "You will never know how much you really believe anything until its truth or falsehood becomes a matter of life and death to you. It is easy to say you believe a rope to be strong and sound as long as you are merely using it to cord a box. But suppose you had to hang by that rope over a precipice. Wouldn't you then first discover how much you really trusted it?" (*A Grief Observed,* 21).

This kind of trust is easily the scariest thing in the world. But when you find the courage to take a leap of faith into the big hands of a good God, you'll finally be able to say from your heart—and not just your head—"Taste and see that the LORD *is* good!" (Ps. 34:8, emphasis added).

17

GOD REQUIRES YOU TO "OWN" YOUR OWN FAITH

Check up on yourselves. Are you really Christians? Do you pass the test? Do you feel Christ's presence and power more and more within you? Or are you just pretending to be Christians when actually you aren't at all?

2 CORINTHIANS 13:5 TLB

When I was about nineteen, four college buddies and I ended up at a men's retreat. Don't ask me how this happened. We were worried about exams and obsessed with girls. Our retreat companions (about 125 gray-haired men, many with pot bellies) were worried about layoffs and the Dow Jones Industrial Average.

I don't remember much about the weekend except the speaker's closing remarks. Speaking from 2 Timothy 4, he was challenging us to finish strong in the Christian life. "Many begin well . . ." he said, "but precious few end well."

Then with all seriousness, he paused for a long, long time and looked out at the audience. Staring hard at us, he said dramatically, "Men, my prayer is that *five* of you will still be walking with God at the end of your lives."

My friends and I were incredulous. Later we talked about that moment: "Five?! Only five?! Heck, there are five of *us!* What about all those old guys? Don't *they* plan to go the distance?"

"Many begin well, but precious few end well." What in the world was the speaker suggesting?

All these years later, I think I know the answer.

There is a phenomenon in the church someone has labeled "borrowed Christianity." It's a common malady. It's what happens when people adopt Christian practices and lingo, but they never quite internalize this faith and make it their own. At least not fully.

This was King Joash's problem (2 Kings 11:1–14:23; 2 Chron. 22:11–25:25). As long as Jehoiada the priest was around to advise him, Joash did good and godly things. The minute Jehoiada died, Joash began to get off track. The shallowness of his faith was quickly revealed.

"Borrowed Christianity" is what you see when people talk *about* God and do stuff *for* God, but they rarely talk *to* God or spend time *with* him. It's a handed-down kind of spirituality, a circumstantial kind of faith. It depends on special events or certain people. In its good moments it can appear healthy and vibrant. In its bad moments it is shown for what it is—a weak and often worthless faith.

Consider: Kevin is from a Christian home. He attended a Christian high school. But now he's a freshman at a large state university. Mom's not there to prod him into going to church on Sunday mornings. His youth director isn't around to nag him about reading his Bible. Professors are challenging some of Kevin's beliefs; dorm neighbors are chuckling at some of Kevin's behaviors (or non-behaviors). Suddenly Kevin is unsure about lots of things. He can still quote many of the Scripture verses he memorized for Bible class, but they seem like mere words.

Kimberly is a twenty-year-old English major who became a Christian the fall semester of her freshman year. If you talked to her for even five minutes, you'd know she's "religious." A closet full of Christian T-shirts, heavy involvement in a campus ministry, a steady stream of Christian music pumping from her CD player. Truth is, Kimberly lives in a little spiritual bubble. In her classes, she sits with Christian friends, at lunch she eats with them, at night she rooms with two of them.

She seems to be a solid Christian. But is she? Both summers she has gone back home to work and has quickly returned to old (bad) habits and unhealthy relationships. Her faith has fizzled. "Why can't I stand up and be strong when I'm away from school?" she laments.

Kevin, Kimberly, and all of us need to realize—or be reminded—that external trappings of "godliness" do not necessarily indicate an internal state of holiness. Activity for God does not equal intimacy with God. A borrowed faith may look strong, but it will not sustain us during the tough times of life.

And so it comes down to this: Do you "own" your own faith? Are you convinced it is true? Or did you just inherit a set of vague beliefs from your parents or pastor? Do you know what you believe? More importantly, do you know *why* you believe what you believe? Is Jesus a real person to you—an ever present savior and friend? Or is he just an idea, a concept? Do your roots go down deep into the soil of God's truth? If not, you won't survive. The winds of adversity and the fickleness of your own heart will pull you away from God and take you places you don't need to go.

It's because most "believers" never wrestle with these questions, never "own" their own faith, that the retreat speaker said, "Many begin well, but precious few end well."

My prayer is that you will be one of those precious few, and that I will be too.

18

LOVING GOD IS *THE* GREAT PRIORITY OF LIFE

One of the teachers of the law came and . . .
asked him, "Of all the commandments,
which is the most important?"
"The most important one," answered Jesus,
"is this: 'Hear, O Israel, the Lord our God,
the Lord is one. Love the Lord your God
with all your heart and with all your soul
and with all your mind and with all your
strength.' The second is this: 'Love your
neighbor as yourself.' There is no
commandment greater than these."

MARK 12:28–31

The great lessons of life often come home to us in the most unusual ways. Like the time during a flag football game my sophomore year when I was confronted with the truth about what matters most in this world.

My roommate and friend, Vernon, was trying to break up a long pass. As he and the larger receiver jumped for the ball, they collided full speed in midair. Vernon got the worse end of the deal. He collapsed in a heap. There in the middle of the intramural playing field he lay motionless. We rushed to his side. He was unconscious but breathing.

After a few moments his eyelids fluttered and he stared up blankly at the sea of faces looking down on him. By now, the intramural director was on the scene.

"Hey, back off! Give the guy some air."

We complied, watching anxiously as the intramural director began to question Vernon.

"What's your name?"

"I don't know. All I know is I love Jesus."

"Do you know where you are?"

"I don't know. All I know is I love Jesus."

"Can you tell me what day this is?"

"I don't know. All I know is I love Jesus."

Again and again, with childlike innocence, Vernon gave the same answer. He wasn't trying to be funny. He certainly wasn't trying to impress anyone with his spirituality. It was as if in those moments, everything trivial had been jarred loose from Vernon's brain. In his dazed state, he was left with only one thing, his core priority, the most important value of all—"All I know is I love Jesus."

We began to laugh, not only out of relief that he was okay, but also at how bizarre the whole scene was. The official didn't quite know what to say. I'm sure he never expected a religious testimony from a concussion victim.

As I reflected on this event later, it occurred to me that in one sense Vernon hadn't been knocked silly at all but rather "knocked sensible"! Sitting there at midfield, seeing stars, he was in touch with a great truth, with *the* great truth. We were telling him to "shake the cobwebs out," yet he seemed to be the one and only person on the whole field at that moment with a clear grasp of what matters most in life.

This story raises questions for us: If we were blindsided (not necessarily on a football field, but by some harsh experience of life), what would that experience reveal about our ultimate values? What matters most to us? What is our ultimate priority? What should it be?

This was, in so many words, the question being posed to Jesus in the passage cited at the beginning of this chapter. The Jews had a very complex code of laws—more than six hundred do's and don'ts. They argued nonstop over which ones should take precedence.

"Boil it down for me, Jesus," the man seemed to be saying. "Of all the things I *could* be giving my life to, what *should* I focus on? I don't want to waste my time on superficial things. I don't want to get to the end of my life and look back with regret. Sum it up. Give it to me in a nutshell."

In essence, Jesus's reply to the man was that utter devotion to God is the highest and best investment we can make. Think about it. What is more fulfilling than knowing the Creator of the universe in an intimate way? Than experiencing his perfect love and loving him back with all that we are? Augustine saw this truth when he prayed, "You have made us for yourself, and our hearts are restless until they can find rest in you." Perhaps this explains how a simple, poor woman like Mother Teresa could find utter delight in a life of total devotion and sacrifice.

But we need more than just a vertical relationship with God. This is why the response of Jesus included loving our neighbors. We were created to move toward others in love, to bless them, and connect with them in God-honoring ways.

Call me silly, but I sometimes think back to that cool fall night when Vernon got his bell rung. And I think about what he kept saying to the intramural official. And I think about that funny, faraway look in his eyes that seemed to be related to something more than just a concussion. And sometimes I almost find myself praying, "God, ring *my* bell like that."

THE **UNOFFICIAL**

19

ONLY GOD CAN FILL THE HOLE IN YOUR SOUL

You don't know quite what it is that you want, but it just fairly makes your heart ache you want it so.

MARK TWAIN

If you scan the sea of students eating lunch in the food court in the middle of campus, you'll find an astonishing variety of people. Each individual is unique, not only in appearance, but also in personality and ability. A wide assortment of interests. Distinct goals. Different dreams.

Pick out a few faces and look at them closely. The guy with the neon baseball cap on backwards—what do you suppose makes him tick? The girl with the gold nose ring—what motivates her to get out of bed in the morning? The couple arguing over by the window—what are they living for?

And are they happy? Or more importantly, are they deeply fulfilled? Do they have a satisfying purpose in life? Do their lives contain an underlying reason for being? Can they honestly say, "I know who I am, why I'm here, and where I'm going"?

For all our differences, we have a few things in common. One of those shared traits is the way in which we pursue meaning. The above quote by Mark Twain says it well. We're hungry—hungry for a kind of "cosmic Happy Meal." That distant rumbling from deep within is our restlessly growling soul. It's saying in so many words, "I'm empty, and I want to be filled."

And so we search. We look for something to give our lives coherence, something to satisfy this relentless appetite. We are a culture of seekers. And sometimes the hunt becomes quite desperate.

If you don't believe me, look around the food court again. If people are not searching for something to fill the emptiness in their souls, then how else do we explain:

- *Mark's secret, shameful five-year addiction to pornography?*
- *Karen's paranoia about being alone, leading to an endless series of boyfriends?*
- *Don's fixation with not making a B, and his detailed plan for med school and beyond?*
- *Helen's willingness to let any and every guy use her for sex?*
- *Kirsten's desperate inability to get even a date, much less a boyfriend?*
- *Catherine's obsession with being thin, prompting her to run long distances daily and to avoid food or to purge when she does eat?*
- *Brandon's total allegiance to his fraternity, even when the members abuse him or ask him to do things he knows are wrong?*

The details vary, but the story is the same. The search for satisfaction is humanity's grand experiment, with ourselves as the guinea pigs. It can be exhilarating to come up with and test a new theory for finding fulfillment. But with each failed test in the laboratory of life, souls get bruised, hearts harden, and cynicism increases.

These are complicated matters about the deepest issues of existence. I don't have any simple solutions for my fellow seekers. But I do know this. I know what the history books tell us about King Solomon. In worldly terms, he had it all or did it all. He was wealthy beyond Bill Gates's wildest dreams. He (apparently) had a pretty active sex life—seven hundred wives and three hundred mistresses, all among the most beautiful women in the world. He was sought after by heads of state for his wisdom and knowledge. His résumé of accomplishments is staggering. He was, simultaneously, an engineering genius, an expert in human nature, a cultural virtuoso, and an administrative marvel.

But if you read Solomon's memoirs, a biblical book entitled Ecclesiastes, what you find is a dissatisfied man. Despite all his blessings, advantages, or whatever you wish to call them, it's clear that even Solomon felt the universal ache of an unfilled soul.

And when all was said and done, when he had concluded his intentional search for meaning and joy in life, he said, rather wistfully, "Here is my final conclusion: Fear God and obey his commands, for this is the duty of every person" (Eccles. 12:13 NLT).

In short, Solomon's message is this: "Take it from a guy who has tried literally everything. Only an intimate relationship with the living God can meet the deepest needs of your heart." Solomon saw, better than most, that in this world God generously gives us wonderful things to enjoy (James 1:17). But if we focus so much on the blessings that we miss the blesser, we will never know true fulfillment.

Question: How then do we come to know God? Answer: Through Jesus Christ (John 14:6). By coming into our world, Jesus the Son showed us what God the Father is like. By dying on a Roman cross, Jesus made a full and final payment for sin, thereby making it possible for rebellious creatures to be forgiven by their righteous Creator. By coming out of the grave, Jesus conquered death, giving us the assurance of eternal life—a fulfilling life that begins the moment we turn to him in faith.

Listen to Jesus, to Solomon, and to C. S. Lewis, who said: "If I find in myself a desire which no experience in this world can satisfy, the most probable explanation is that I was made for another world" (*Mere Christianity*, 120).

You want disappointment? Keep chasing the illusions of this world. You want ultimate fulfillment? It can be yours when you realize you were created by God for God, and when you put your life completely in his hands.

20

GOD HAS DEFEATED OUR GREAT ENEMY

There are two equal and opposite errors into which our race can fall about the devils. One is to disbelieve in their existence. The other is to believe, and to feel an excessive and unhealthy interest in them.

C. S. LEWIS

A few years ago, North American Christians were buzzing about an intriguing novel called *This Present Darkness*. Penned by Frank Peretti, a former ski maker, the book tells the story of the intense spiritual warfare in a small college town.

Though not intended to be a definitive textbook on demonic and angelic activity, the book neverthe-less caused shock waves by its unique approach. It allowed the reader to "see" these invisible spirit beings fighting with one another over the lives of very real people. Most people who finished the book became more convinced of the truth of spiritual warfare and much more serious about their prayer lives. I know I did.

Since that time, our whole culture has become obsessed with angels and all things supernatural. Many people seem to be convinced (or at least hopeful) that there are indeed spiritual realities that transcend this life.

Guess what? This is precisely what the Bible has been saying all along. From the opening chapters of Genesis to the final page of Revelation, the Scripture depicts the truth of intense cosmic combat—God the Creator together with his angelic armies engaged in an all-out war with Satan and the other fallen angels (now called demons). Human souls are the sought-after spoils in this universal conflict. And planet earth is the battle ground.

According to the Bible, the outcome of the war is not in doubt. In a crazy, difficult-to-comprehend way, the death and resurrection of Christ proved to be the deciding battle. Full of foolish hatred, the devil unwittingly played right into God's hands by killing Jesus. In doing so, he made it possible for sin to be forgiven, and for sinners to be reconciled to God.

Thus, the cross was Satan's Waterloo, his Trojan Horse, his Hiroshima, meaning—if you dozed your way through history—the war is over. The devil and his troops have been defeated. Certain judgment awaits. Nevertheless, like a stubborn, never-say-die kamikaze pilot, Satan refuses to wave the white flag. He is determined to fight to the death (his own), and he is committed to taking as many people down with him as possible.

What does all this mean to you as you prepare to launch out into the world?

First, it means you need to be *prepared*.

Your enemy is real. According to the Bible, he is a master tempter (Gen.

3:1–5; Matt. 4:1), a consummate deceiver (John 8:44; 2 Cor. 11:14), as well as a ruthless murderer (John 8:44).

Make no mistake about it. The devil hates you. He wants to destroy your life. This is why Peter warns us in his first epistle to "be self-controlled and alert" (5:8). A lot of people much smarter and sharper and more "spiritual" than either you or I have fallen into the enemy's devastating traps. The solution? Use the heavenly armor that God has provided for his children (Eph. 6:13–18). Then, don't lower your guard, not even for a minute.

Second, the reality of cosmic conflict means you need to be *committed*.

In this great war, there is no such thing as neutrality. You can't be a spiritual "Switzerland." Jesus said bluntly, "He who is not with me is against me, and he who does not gather with me scatters" (Matt. 12:30). In other words, we must declare which side we are on. Otherwise we are like the proverbial Civil War soldier who wore a blue jacket and gray pants—and ended up getting shot at by both sides!

Third, you can be *encouraged*.

Though Satan has great power, God has *all* power. He is infinitely greater than the devil (1 John 4:4). Since God dwells within all who have put their faith in Christ, we have ample power to resist the tempter (James 4:7; 1 Peter 5:9). And we can rejoice in the great truth of Romans 16:20: "The God of peace will soon crush Satan under your feet."

When I'm under heavy attack, that's a verse I quote often!

THE **UNOFFICIAL**

Truths about the Rest of Your Life

21

GOOD THINGS COME TO THOSE WHO WAIT

Everyone is just waiting.
NO!
That's not for you!
Somehow you'll escape all that
waiting and staying.

DR. SEUSS

Think about how much of your life you spend waiting. At stoplights. At fast-food drive-thru windows. In lines. (A really time-efficient college student could read the complete works of Russian novelist Fyodor Dostoyevsky in the time he or she will spend standing and staring at the backs of other peoples' heads over the next four to five years.) For test results. For the mail. For the weekend. For graduation. To get asked out. To move out. To get married.

Despite our culture's best attempts to reduce the time we spend waiting (microwave ovens, instant oatmeal, home pregnancy tests, overnight shipping, one-hour photo processing, express checkouts, and so on), waiting is still an ever present fact of life. And we are impatient people. We hate to wait . . . which explains why we are so susceptible to the lure of instant gratification.

What exactly is instant gratification? It is that alluring promise that comes to us in various forms, and claims, "You don't have to wait. You can have whatever you want, and you can have it right now." For instance, if you decide you "need" money or want some expensive possession, you can apply for—and receive, almost instantly—easy credit. Maybe you've already had banks and credit card companies practically beg you to apply for one of their cards. (If not, be aware that such a day is just ahead.) Gone are the days of working hard and saving your money and paying as you go. Today it's "buy now, pay later," often with the added bonus of "no payments and no interest for twelve months!"

Instant gratification is what's behind the temptation to sleep with someone before marriage or the decision to marry the first person who comes along. It promises wonderful things now . . . while it conveniently leaves out the part about there being a heavy price to pay later.

Waiting might not be fun, but we should note that it is biblical. From Genesis to Revelation, saints had to wait. There's Noah working on his giant floating zoo, waiting for something called rain. A few pages later we find the story of Abraham and Sarah, each with one foot in the grave (or at least the nursing home), finally having the child God had promised twenty-five years earlier! The entire Old Testament pictures Israel waiting and longing for the long-expected Messiah. A common theme in the New Testament is that of Christians waiting eagerly for the return of Jesus Christ. Hebrews 11 is a gallery of godly people who opted to trust God and wait for him to work, rather than rushing ahead and doing foolish things in their own power.

Waiting, annoying and frustrating though it is, builds character in us. Contrary to the counsel of Dr. Seuss, it *is* for us. We develop patience as we exercise self-control in waiting. We develop inner strength that enables us to say no or not yet to impulsive urges and overeager hormones. We learn to trust God as we go (often alone) against the flow of a generation that has deemed "wait" to be the ultimate four-letter word. In waiting, we live out the truth that God is God and we are not. Contrary to the common worldly advice, "Don't just sit there . . . do something!" we hear the whisper of God's Spirit, "Don't do anything just yet. Just sit there for now. Wait. Trust me." And so we put our lives in his hands and subject ourselves to his timetable and plan. And in the end, where it really matters, we find blessings that far surpass the glittery but short-lived rewards of instant gratification.

I was talking with a student a few weeks ago, and we were discussing his relationship with (and impending engagement to) a wonderful Christian woman. He reminisced about a previous relationship, which a lot of friends had encouraged, but which he had felt wasn't right. When he suddenly broke things off, he caught a lot of flak. And he was forced to re-enter the dating scene.

But smiling, he noted, "I'm glad I didn't just settle for that first relationship. I'm so glad I waited. For this much obedience [and saying this, he spread his thumb and forefinger apart about two inches], I got so much more."

What was he saying? Simply this: Good things come to those who wait.

Don't settle for less than the best. Keep waiting until God decides, in his perfect time, to give you things beyond your wildest dreams (Eph. 3:20).

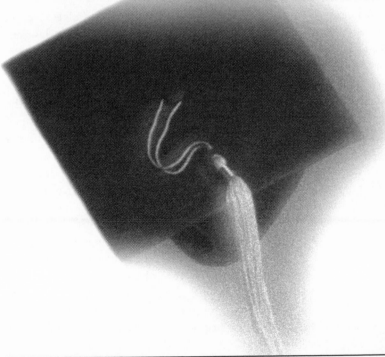

22

GOOD THINGS COME TO THOSE WHO WORK

All hard work brings a profit,
but mere talk leads only to poverty.

PROVERBS 14:23

Just what kind of a college student was I? Well, I'll just say this: I believed in working smart, not hard.

For instance, when I found out my major required three semesters of a foreign language, I quickly enrolled in Latin. Why Latin? Because it is one of the so-called "dead" languages. No longer spoken, Latin does not require frequent trips to the language lab to listen to sleep-inducing audiotapes. While all my friends were perfecting their French and Spanish accents, I was merely concentrating on the written words in my *Lingua Latina* textbook. Smart, eh? I made A's and B's learning cool phrases like *corpus delecti* and *tempus fugit* . . . which, unfortunately, I can no longer translate.

Another time, in an upper level journalism class, our professor (also an investigative reporter for a local TV station) decided our entire class should make a video documentary about suspected drug smuggling in the Port of Baton Rouge. What better way to learn the process of newsgathering, acquire expertise in using a real TV camera, become adept at conducting interviews and editing video than by producing a thirty-minute broadcast? With our instructor's guidance and experience, this would be an awesome chance to get some actual, hands-on TV news training. And with his ties to the station, he could guarantee our story would be aired and that we would make valuable contacts.

Did I take advantage of this marvelous opportunity? No way! It sounded like way too much work. Besides, early in the planning stages of the project, the instructor announced he was looking for an ancient movie about drug abuse called *Reefer Madness,* a film containing some cheesy clips he wanted to include in our class documentary. Smiling broadly, I pulled the professor aside after class. "I can get that film for you."

He was euphoric. "If you can get a copy of that movie, you have an automatic A in the class! You don't even have to show up the rest of the semester."

I promptly left campus, rented the old movie reel from a little-known shop in town, dropped it by my professor's office, and never attended another class. As promised, I got my A. Easily worth the twenty-dollar rental price of the film, don't you agree?

"Take the path of least resistance." That was my motto in school. Why knock yourself out, I reasoned, if a minimal effort is good enough?

Over the years I've learned that my approach was (and is) the rule rather than the exception. Most students opt for the easy way out. Non-students do too. Why is that? Why is it that the path of least resistance is the path with the most travelers? Are we lazy? Afraid? Slaves of peer pressure?

I suspect the truth involves all of those things. Because we live

THE **UNOFFICIAL**

under the illusion that life is supposed to be easy (see chap. 1), we are not willing to work very hard. Unlike our grandparents, who grew up in an era of hard times and hard work, where the catch-phrase was "If-you-want-it-you're-gonna-have-to-work-your-tail-off-for-it!" the last couple of generations—mine and yours—have had things handed to us on the proverbial silver platter. We are soft. We believe good things should happen to us if we make even a minimal effort. Furthermore, we are afraid to take chances. Why enroll in the course you might make a D in if you can just as easily take the class that is an automatic A? Why work hard and spend long hours learning a skill you don't actually need right now when you could be taking it easy? That's what most of our friends are doing. Why should we pursue a different course?

Here's why: The path of least resistance—attractive though it is at the time—is the path of least rewards. The Bible speaks clearly about the value and blessing of hard work. We are called to avoid laziness and to seek to honor God in all that we do (Col. 3:23). Only the hard-working, faithful servants win the Lord's commendation (Luke 19:11–27).

Remember all my brilliant schemes in college to avoid having to exert myself, like taking Latin—the easiest language? Yeah, well, a lot of good Latin did me on multiple mission trips south of the border and to France! (Imagine my surprise when I realized they don't speak Latin in Latin America!) I could kick myself for not learning a useful language. And my "purchased" journalism grade is worthless too. What good is an A if you don't learn anything in the class? I would have been far better off immersing myself in the class project. Who knows, I might be a top network reporter today, or at least have my own talk show ("College students who flush live animals down dormitory toilets—on the next 'Len'").

In closing let me say, *"Veni, vedi, vinci,"* which is Latin for "I went to college and majored in journalism, and I don't even know how to program my VCR."

23

TODAY WILL
HAPPEN ONLY
ONCE

Wherever you are, be all there.

JIM ELLIOT

At age twenty-one, I decided to take a personality test. (This was after a woman I was dating began telling other people that, as far as she was concerned, I did not have a personality.)

It was one of those mail-order things. I sent away for it ("for the low price of only thirty-five dollars"), completed it at home, mailed it back, and four to six weeks later received a computerized printout ("in a handsome brown binder") describing what the test revealed about my unique temperament.

I still remember the first question. It asked me to draw three circles describing how I viewed the past, the present, and the future. I thought briefly and drew a medium-sized circle representing the past, a small circle representing the present, and an extra-large circle representing the future.

What this test later taught me was that, for whatever reasons, I was so preoccupied with the past, and

THE **UNOFFICIAL**

so obsessed with the future, that I was neglecting all that was taking place in the present. I was going through my days physically present but emotionally absent. I was merely going through the motions of living.

Years later I saw the movie *Dead Poets' Society*, which popularized the phrase *carpe diem*. With my extensive Latin training (see chap. 22), I was able to translate it immediately: "Carp taste better when they are panfried in cornmeal the same day they are seized." Or, as Robin Williams expressed it, far less poetically and much more loosely, "Seize the day."

That's what we're talking about here. Seizing the day. Living in the now. Being fully alive. Treasuring the wonderful gift of life that God has blessed you with this moment.

Psychologist Abraham Maslow once said, "I can feel guilty about the past, apprehensive about the future, but only in the present can I act. The ability to be in the present moment is a major component of mental wellness."

It's true that life is hard (see chap. 1). It's right to remember that we are fallen creatures in a fallen world (see chap. 7). It's fitting to keep one eye on eternity, to "set [our] minds on things above" (Col. 3:2). But it's also biblical to live with a sense of wonder and awe.

Do you grasp the truth that this particular day will happen only once? This marvelous day filled with so many good things: the smell of approaching rain or the scent of great cologne, the taste of Cookies & Cream ice cream or fajitas, an unexpected phone call from an old friend, the opportunity to encourage a neighbor who's lonely, the sunset, the flicker of a candle, the sound of the waves on the beach, the lizard that climbs up the side of the tub while you're soaking in a hot bath and licks the Ivory soap and begins blowing bubbles (Don't laugh! This actually happened to me right after I graduated!).

Life happens so fast. Each day and every week are filled with unique moments and wonderful occasions. When they're gone, you can never get them back. So look for the one-of-a-kind opportunities all around. Enjoy each moment. Take pleasure in the many blessings of today.

Because it will happen only once.

24

CONFLICTS DON'T MAGICALLY GO AWAY

I don't like to face problems head on. . . .
In fact, this is a distinct philosophy of mine.
No problem is so big or so complicated
that it can't be run away from!
LINUS, IN THE COMIC STRIP *PEANUTS*

Since Heather and Karen were best friends in high school, they decided to get an apartment together after graduation. The girls' troubles began within days of signing a lease.

Almost immediately, Heather began to notice that Karen is not the neatest person in the world. Karen routinely stacks her dirty dishes in the sink. Heather lets them pile up for a day or so. Eventually, however, the mess bugs her so much, she washes the dishes, mumbling under her breath, "Karen is such an inconsiderate slob!" One day Heather watched Karen miss the garbage can with a disposable razor. She decided to see how long her messy roommate would let it sit there. We're at day sixty-six and counting.

In retaliation (although she wouldn't call it that), Heather periodically helps herself to Karen's ample food supply in the freezer and pantry. Several times, Karen has come home from work only to find that the food she was envisioning for supper is gone.

Since they moved in, Karen has kept the air conditioner running. Meanwhile Heather has fretted over high utility bills. This explains how the silent "war of the thermostat" began. Karen comes in and puts it on the "North Pole" setting. When she leaves, Heather turns it back to the "Death Valley" mark. Back and forth it goes. But no one ever says a thing.

So . . . as you can probably guess, things are tense in Shadow Lake Apartment #134. The girls barely speak anymore. They're civil to each other, but just barely. On her way home from work, Karen often finds herself hoping that Heather's car will not be in the parking lot. Every time she pulls in and sees it sitting there, her heart sinks.

Heather, on the other hand, has told her mom about the unpleasant situation.

"So why don't you just talk to Karen? She's your friend."

"Aw, Mom, it's too complicated. Besides, our lease is up in another three months. I'll just endure till then and try to find a new roommate."

I confess that during my college experience I was an expert in the art of conflict avoidance. If a friend or roommate bugged me, I clammed up. If a girlfriend hurt me, I pouted silently. I swept grievances under the rug. I stuffed unpleasant emotions deep within my soul. *It's not a big deal,* I would try to reason internally. *Why rock the boat? I should just blow it off and move on.*

But one can only do that for so long. Eventually the pressure inside builds until something minor triggers a violent explosion. Unresolved irritations lead to uncontrolled outbursts—raised voices, pointing fingers, hurtful accusations, and name-calling. Things can get volatile—even between close friends.

What was my problem? What is Heather's and Karen's? A skewed view of conflict, not to mention inadequate skills in dealing with it. Over time, wiser roommates and mentors taught me these seven valuable principles:

1. *Conflict is inevitable.* When fallen, unique, quirky people interact, there will *always* be disagreements. The only way to completely avoid conflict is to live alone in a cave in the remote regions of Outer Slobovia (not my idea of a good time). Once you accept the truth that conflict is a fact of life, you will no longer be "blown away" when it happens.
2. *Conflict is not inherently bad.* Granted, working through a disagreement is not fun. Who wants to bring up unpleasant issues? But experience has shown me time and again that honestly talking things out leads to better understanding and new perspectives, if not richer relationships.
3. *You should take the initiative to resolve conflicts.* Let's face it, we all want to be pleasant and nice. We want people to like us. That's why we avoid conflict and pretend everything is okay—even when it's not. But if we wait for others to take the first step, we'll spend our lives waiting! Romans 12:18 says, "If it is possible, as far as it depends on *you*, live at peace with everyone" (emphasis added).
4. *There are commonsense rules for conflict resolution.*

   - *Be Spirit-filled. Can you imagine the difference if your life was marked by the qualities listed in Galatians 5:22–23?*
   - *Be prayerful. Ask God for the strength to control your emotions, the wisdom to know what to say and how to say it, and the courage to speak up.*
   - *Be timely. Don't drag your feet. Allowing too much time to elapse creates opportunities for bitterness and resentment to build (Eph. 4:26).*
   - *Be careful. If you feel yourself starting to lose your temper, call a time-out for a few minutes or until you can once again talk calmly.*
   - *Be sensitive. Listen to what the other person or persons are saying. Try to put yourself in their shoes.*
   - *Be fair. Avoid loaded language such as "you always" or "you never." Stick to the subject at hand. If the conflict arose because you borrowed clothes without asking, don't bring up their habit of leaving dirty dishes.*

THE **UNOFFICIAL**

- *Be honest.* We are called to speak the truth in love (Eph. 4:15).
- *Be gentle.* Your calmness can help defuse situations in which others are tense and heated (Prov. 15:1).
- *Be wise.* Not every disagreement is worthy of your attention (Prov. 17:14). If your roommate likes country music and you like jazz, that's not worth arguing over. The volume of the music might be a problem worth discussing or the times when it is played, but personal tastes are a whole different issue.
- *Be humble.* When your behavior has been selfish or inconsiderate, own up to it and ask forgiveness. "I'm sorry; I was wrong" are perhaps the five most powerful words when resolving conflicts.

5. *The goal in conflict resolution should be God's glory and our unity.* Often we approach a conflict not as a problem to be solved but as a battle to be won. But what good is it to win an argument if, in the process, you lose a friendship? When you stop trying to win arguments and start trying to win friends, you're on the right track.

6. *Learning to resolve conflict now will save you much heartache down the road.* I know a lot of miserable married couples. Why are they so unhappy? At least in part because they have never learned to resolve conflict. Marriage is a breeding ground for tension. That doesn't mean it's bad. Not at all! Marriage is wonderful! But only if you know how to work through conflicts. It's best for you to hone your skills now with parents, friends, and roommates.

7. *Sometimes you have to agree to disagree.* In a perfect world, we'd resolve every conflict to everyone's complete satisfaction. But we don't live in a perfect world. Sometimes we can't find common ground. And that's okay. In those instances we must refrain from the temptation to argue about differences, and we must concentrate instead on areas of agreement. The mistake so many make is to cave in against their better judgment. Generally, the pushier person with the stronger personality wins. It's not good to be stubborn, but it's not healthy to be a doormat either.

Please hear me. Save yourself a lot of grief. Realize that time *doesn't* heal all wounds. Ignoring a conflict doesn't make it go away. You have to address it. And if you don't make it a priority to learn and practice this skill, I'll tell it to you straight: You're in for one unpleasant life.

25

IT'S NEVER TOO LATE TO TURN AROUND

If your sin were too great for his grace, he never would have saved you in the first place. Your temptation isn't late-breaking news in heaven. Your sin doesn't surprise God. He saw it coming. Is there any reason to think that the One who received you the first time won't receive you every time?

MAX LUCADO

One of my roommates in college, let's call him Dave, was also one of my best friends. We struggled to know God together. We prayed, read the Bible, and went on summer outreach projects together.

About the time of my graduation, Dave married. He got a well-paying job, and the happy newlyweds joined a church in a neighboring community where Dave became a very active leader.

Storybook life. At least that's how it appeared to the rest of us. The whole thing seemed too good to be true. It wasn't long before we discovered it was. There were deep problems in the marriage and deeper struggles in Dave's life.

THE **UNOFFICIAL**

About a year into the marriage, Dave suddenly left his wife. He cut off all contact with his fellow church members and Christian friends. When we heard he had moved in with a girl not yet out of high school, we elected a representative to try to reason with him. But Dave wouldn't talk or listen. His mind was made up. He and his new girlfriend moved away. Last we heard, Dave was living in Southern California. That was at least eight years ago.

A few months back, shortly after I got Internet access, I found a service that helps you locate "lost" people. I immediately thought of Dave and typed in his full name. If the information my modem retrieved is correct, I think I now know where Dave lives.

I want to call him. I don't know what he'd say. For that matter, I'm not sure what I'd say. It's been at least fifteen years since we've had any contact. Maybe Dave has come back to God. I hope and pray that's the case. But I also know that when you make wrong choices, it's easy to slip so deeply into sin and guilt that you feel as though God hates you. When you get to that point, despair can keep you running for a long time. Some people never stop fleeing.

Suppose I dialed the number and Dave answered, what would I say? I've thought about that a lot. If he's still running from God—and if he'd stay on the phone with me—I would want to remind him of all the people in the Bible who were once where he is.

I'd tell him about wicked King Manasseh (2 Chron. 33:1–20), who, among other awful things, took his own precious sons and sacrificed them in pagan rituals to false gods! Then I'd point him to the passage that says Manasseh humbled himself and asked the Lord for mercy. And how that plea, filled with grief and remorse, moved the very heart of God. Hard though it is to believe, even Manasseh found forgiveness and a fresh start.

I'd tell him about all the others too. The prodigal son who nearly broke his dad's heart (Luke 15:11–31), the woman at the well with a long history of live-in lovers (John 4:7–26), the woman caught in the very act of adultery (John 8:1–11), the thief on the cross (Luke 23:39–43). The Bible is full of stories like that—people whose wrecked and apparently hopeless lives were totally turned around by the grace and mercy of God. That's the gospel, the Good News: Anyone, repeat *anyone*—Dave, you, me—can start all over.

If you're running from God, for whatever reason, you need to know that it's never too late to turn around. Never.

Now, if you'll excuse me, I have a phone call to make.

LEN WOODS is a husband, dad, and pastor in Ruston, Louisiana. He is the former editor of *Youthwalk,* a contributor to the *Nelson Study Bible,* and the author of *Life Application Family Devotions, Tough Choices Men Face,* and *I'm Outta Here!* for which he won a Gold Medallion Award.